# Once Upon a Blue Moon

## Olivia Norfolk

*Dr Olivia Norfolk was a rising star in ecological research whose achievements laid the foundation for what promised to be an extraordinary career. She was a gifted writer and educator, and a passionate advocate for the role of traditional agriculture in conservation. Her loss to the field of ecology is immense but her life's work will have a lasting impact.*

*A place has the power to affect people.*

*This is my story about the mountains of South Sinai, of the little town of St Katherine which has changed my life. It is a tale about magic and madness, of friendship and love. It is based on my own memories, fallible as they may be, and from the tales of people that I chanced upon.*

*The book is dedicated to all of those who I have met along the way, who have shared and shaped my experiences, and who too have been touched by the power of that sacred landscape.*

*Some of the names have been changed.*

# OLD WORLD

*White desert*

# 2009

*Olivia in Sinai*

# Chapter 1

The sun beat down on the carpenter and his wife. He wiped his weathered brow where pools of dirty sweat had gathered. His wife sighed heavily and leaned her head into the neck of the donkey. The journey was long and the three had grown weary. They had been walking for three months now. The once familiar darkness of the German Black Forest had been replaced by the oppressive heat of the Syrian steppe. "Not far now," mumbled the carpenter towards the horizon. Only seven hundred miles until they would emerge from the expansive desert, drawn upwards into the mountains of St Katherine.

They say his wife died on the way. Either that or she came to her senses and left him. All I can be sure of is that the carpenter and the donkey survived their epic journey. To this day the aged German hippie and his faithful beast can be found living contentedly in a handmade wooden shack at the base of Wadi Shraig. Tonight, the crescent moon hovers above them as they sleep. The billion stars glitter brightly in the black night sky. The valley is silent. Only as you move towards the road will you hear the steady tread of the procession of camels which make their way towards the monastery. These camels do not carry wise men but are ridden by entrepreneurial Bedouin boys who spend the nights touting for business at the base of Mount Sinai.

From the road you can make out the glow of the iconic Fox Camp sign. At this hour the camp is deserted, but wait a while, and you will hear the excited whispers of tourists preparing for their torch-lit ascent of the holy mountain. Meander through the olive grove and you will pass a cave full of cats and a lone man, Kevin. He lies curled amongst his feline companions, dreaming of dancing with dolphins atop Glastonbury Tor.

The hot August night has driven me outside in search of a breeze. I have dragged the mattress from my room and now lie beneath the trees. Mosquitoes hum around me as I gaze at the stars and wait for sleep to come.

My first visit to St Katherine was over a decade ago. I was young, an undergraduate carrying out ecological research for my dissertation project. I was excited but also nervous about spending a month in the Sinai desert, imagining windswept sand dunes, Arabian Nights and camels. I was right about the camels but little else. When our minibus pulled into the Fox Camp carpark I was surprised by the imposing peak of the Ras es-Safsafeh mountain which loomed over us. In the evening darkness, the mountains seemed ominous, but I would soon learn to love the way in which those peaks guard the small town that lies nestled amongst them, creating a sense of intimacy and protection of this place that I would one day call home

Of course I had done some research before we came, reading about ecological sampling techniques and the biology of the lizards that we hoped to study, but it simply had not occurred to me to research the place itself. I knew little about this town's history, its culture or its spirituality. What I did know had been gleaned from the storybooks of my childhood. I had heard the tales of Moses, learned about the plagues of locusts and the rivers of blood, of how he led his people across the desert and parted the Red Sea. It was here, on the slopes that rise up behind the camp, that he encountered a burning bush that spoke to him, guiding him upwards. Up there, just beyond the crown of Ras es-Safsafeh, Moses had stood amidst the lightning and the thunder, and received the Ten Commandments from his Lord.

Across the road from the camp stretches the plain of Wadi Raheh, where the crowds once gathered to hear Moses read God's words from the tablets of stone: "Thou Shalt Not Steal, Thou Shalt Not Covet Your Neighbour's Wife, Thou Shalt Not Bear False Witness Against Thy Neighbour." Tonight, in their place, the lights of the Plaza Hotel glow in the darkness. In the foyer a group of Chinese tourists huddles, preparing for the climb. A mile or so down the road a queue of coaches is forming outside St Katherine Monastery, where the Bedouin boys and their camels are waiting. A young Russian girl steps off a coach and shivers, regretting her outfit choice. The pink shorts and strappy top that suited the beaches of Sharm El Sheikh do not work so well here, in the cool mountain air.

Most nights you will find a similar scene, with people from across the world gathering in preparation for the starlit ascent to the summit of Mount Sinai. Tonight, they are tourists, here for the history, and to take in the views. But they are following an ancient pilgrimage route that has been used for centuries, when pilgrims from Jewish, Christian and Islamic faiths gathered together at the summit to pay homage at the site where Moses received the word of God. The climb is steep and tough for those tourists not used to the rocky terrain, taking perhaps three or more hours. They travel one by one, forming a procession that snakes its way up through the darkness.

The Bedouin guides lead the way, offering camel rides for those who are tiring; to the old and the frail; and to those dressed in flip-flops or heels. But when they near the top, the guides hang back, gossiping and laughing, as the visitors go on alone. This final clamber to the peak must be done on foot, one final surge of effort up the Steps of Penance—a steep, narrow staircase of stone, hand-carved into the mountain itself. Just seven hundred and fifty more steps to climb, and then you will have made it to the summit of Mount Sinai. The mountain of Moses, also known as Jebel Musa.

Those who have arrived in time sit huddled now, as the sun begins to creep up behind the horizon. The world stretches out before them, the seemingly endless mountain massif shimmering in pale pinks and blues that dissolve into the distant haze. Everyone is quiet, unified by the transient beauty of the moment. But the sun marches onwards, first a glimpse of orange on the horizon, soon a glowing sphere of gold. And then the spell is broken. It is time to get on with the day.

# Chapter 2

"Wakey wakey, rise and shine!" bellows Professor Benkhe as he marches back and forth past the sleeping students. It is early dawn; the tourists have taken their photos and are heading back down to the coaches that will return them to their resorts on the coast.

I yawn and extract myself from my mosquito net and begin to get ready for a day out in the mountains. There are ten of us in total, most working with the Professor on a project examining the spatial distribution of rodent parasites. Since this involves even earlier starts to check and empty rodent traps, followed by long hours in the makeshift lab rifling through the poor little creatures' gut contents, I am happy to be studying the behaviour and ecology of a charismatic lizard, known as the Sinai Agama.

I am working with another student, Alice, and, as is tradition here, we are accompanied each day by a Bedouin guide from the local tribe. His name is Muhammad, and he shows us the way through the mountain trails. By now, two-weeks into our stay, we have established a familiar routine, our days filled with stories and jokes.

The lizards that we are searching for are only active in the warmth of the day so, unlike the other students who go out in the cool of the early mornings and evenings, we must walk in the heat of the midday sun. We climb, we scan the red granite rocks around us on the look-out for the lizards. When we spot them, we observe them for quarter of an hour recording their behaviour, what they do, where they go, what they eat.

Sounds simple, but each time I see one I have to resist the urge to creep up close and get a proper look. Instead, we must step away and watch from afar through binoculars to avoid disturbing them.

What makes the Sinai Agama really special is its colour. The rusty brown running from the crown of its head to the tip of its tail merges seamlessly into the rock. From above, through the eyes of a circling raptor, the lizard is invisible but from ground height you might catch a glimpse of intense, vivid blue. If you are lucky, the entire face, throat, legs and belly will shine, sparkling against the red granite, a gem of turquoise. This fast, agile lizard has the ability to change colour in front of your very eyes; bright blue when it wants to be seen, but dissolving, chameleon-like, into the rock when under threat.

This particular morning, we head towards the village before veering upwards into Wadi Arbien. Translated as Valley of Forty, this wide, steep-sided valley is named after the forty Cypress trees that once grew here. Now only a dozen or so remain, standing tall amongst the olive groves.

Our route takes us upwards, past the high stone walls that enclose the monastery-owned garden, past the garden of Ramadan, a Bedouin man who lives there with his family, and out on to the high crest of the mountain. It is a steady climb, several hours when factoring in observations of lizards, and the sweat has started trickling down my back. I am grateful when Muhammad pauses about half-way up, beckoning us into the shade. As Alice and I glug down our water, Muhammad taps at a rock next to us and begins telling a story.

"Many years before, a long time before now—" he pauses for effect, "—there was a man who walked here, a man called

Musa. Musa carried with him a tall stick, and he hit the rock with this stick." He taps the centre of the boulder. "And made water come out."

I get up and place my palm across the smooth, worn stone as so many have done before me and imagine the cool water gushing through my fingers.

"A miracle," I murmur.

It feels strange to hear this Arabic man telling the Biblical tales of Moses as if they were his own, but of course they are. Or rather they belong here. To the mountains.

We continue up, emerging from the valley onto the mountain ridge, where the crystal-clear sky opens up around us. Instead of following the path of Moses, up to the peak of Jebel Musa, we take a sharp left, cutting down into a parallel valley which will lead us back to Fox Camp.

The wadi is wider here, with wildflowers poking their heads from the sandy floor, but it soon narrows, becoming steep and rocky. The scramble down is a challenge, but it is worth it for the view. Terraced gardens lie hidden like gems amongst the barren rocks, their trees laden with almonds and figs. From under their canopy comes the buzz of bees and the sweet scent of wild mint.

An old woman watches from the steep valley sides, puzzling over the two Western girls as they point excitedly at something within a pile of rocks. She notes Muhammad, her neighbour's brother, who takes a seat beneath the shade of a nearby rock. They move and laugh with such freedom and she cannot help but wonder how their experiences of womanhood have differed from her own. Then, sighing, she gets up, wraps her black scarf tighter around her face and calls for her goats, who are scattered across the rock-face. Slowly, she leads the goats back along the uneven trail towards the village and the small, simple house she calls home.

Alice and I spend the next fifteen minutes watching the lizard we have found, which sits stubbornly in the crack of a rock. The minutes drag by. The blue lizard perfectly still, sitting patiently while I begin fidgeting and dreaming about the cool shower and dinner that awaits me back at camp.

Finally, my stop-watch beeps, signalling that the observation period is over and the lizard darts away. "Yalla Beena! Let's go!" calls Muhammad, equally keen to get home for the day.

That evening all the students gather in the *arisha*, a circular stone hut that serves as the camp's dining area. This is the time for swapping stories from the day, finding out how many mice were caught or who struggled with the sight of rodent guts.

Outside, Kevin sits alone in the olive grove, his roll-up cigarette glowing in the darkness. The laughter and chatter drifts towards him across the warm night air and he inhales deeply, his face crumpling with the effort. For a moment, he floats away from here, transported to another, simpler world.

Inside the hut dinner is served, with the Chef Radwan placing steaming plates of sticky rice and fried chicken on the low tables in front of us. A black cat begins pacing, back and forth, his fierce eyes focused on the prize.

"His name is Dinosaur," says Kevin, entering the hut and crouching down on the floor beside me.

Kevin's voice is soft, almost child-like, and he looks weary. His long brown hair hangs limply around his unshaven face and his wide eyes are fixed on the food. I look at the cat, whose muscles ripple as he prowls, and nod.

"I can understand why," I reply.

Kevin has clutched his knees to his chest and started rocking, slowly, forwards then back. Unlike the cat, he is thin, his T-shirt worn and ripped, dusty trousers hanging from his body. The trousers gathered at the waist, kept up only by an old piece of string.

Kevin is not a Bedouin, nor a tourist, but a full-time resident of Fox Camp. How he survives is unclear to him and to those around him, but odd jobs around the camp keep him fed and watered. He grew up in England, surrounded by the green hills of home, but was drawn here by the Monastery and the mountain and does not have it in him to leave.

As the days and weeks pass, I get to know Kevin better. He is often found wandering around the camp, heading to the village or gathering food scraps for the cats. When we sit together, he talks about distant memories from home, his lost love, and the power of the spiritual world.

He is at his most animated when talking about the Shamans of South America and his plan to take part in their traditional *Iowasca* ceremony. The ceremony will take place in the dead of night, with the Shaman brewing tea from forest vines with psychedelic properties.

A few sips of the divine *Iowasca*, and the spirit is freed from the body, floating upwards into the rainforest canopy, dancing with the plants and animals, becoming one with the elements, the rock, rain, and air. Kevin disappears when he tells these stories, drifting into a world of his imagination. When he emerges it is with sadness, a painful realisation that his dream might not come to pass.

Most days Kevin feels lost and aimless, but today he is motivated. He has organized a pottery class for the students and plans to teach them how to craft their own ocarinas out of clay. First, he lays out a large rug, before placing down the bucket of clay that he has sourced from the coast. When the students arrive, Kevin becomes absorbed in the task of teaching, showing them how to shape and mold the clay into a hollow shell, to extend the mouthpiece and create adornments, such as the wings and beak of a bird. It is satisfying to see the foundations of these simple clay wind instruments taking shape, but the real magic happens when the ocarinas come back from the kiln two week later ready for tuning.

There is something incredible about creating music from an inanimate lump of clay, and now the ocarinas are returned, our masterpieces fired and cured, Kevin shows us how to create the holes and we begin. When he is not coaxing tunes from our ocarinas, he waters the newly planted eucalyptus saplings at the coach park at the edge of the village, where Farag is building a restaurant and gift shop to squeeze money from the day-tripping holiday makers who visit from the beach resorts of Sharm El Sheik. This is just the start of my adventures, snatched memories wrested from my past. Every place has the power to affect people, and this place, Fox Camp, the mountains of South Sinai, and the little town of St Katherine's, are those which changed my life. I will tell you a tale about magic and madness, of friendship and love, and I dedicate to all those I have met along the way, who have shared and shaped my experiences, like we shaped the little ocarinas, and who too have been shaped by the power of this sacred landscape.

I will tell you about shared dinners, the cat Dinosaur and the music Kevin has in his soul. There will be masters and gardens, changes to the camp. You will learn more of Mohammed, the computer room, and flicking seashells.

You will see the star-flooded nights and hear Kevin playing the viola.

There will be Carlos, Qasim, Farag and the sea, and Hamdi on the roof.

I will get my PhD and tell you all about Beth and Abdul, desert parties and moonlight.

You might laugh at the American girl, and my attempts at yoga, and Uncle Soliman.

Once upon a blue moon great things happen, and great things happened to me.

Listen carefully and I will tell you how I came to discover the bee that will carry my name, forever.

# 2010

*"The Tent", Fox Camp's meeting place*

# Chapter 3

In Fox Camp things are constantly changing. Though the camp is built upon land with an ancient and deep-rooted history, on the surface there is continual adaptation, expansion, and change. Farag Fox, the camp owner, is acutely aware of the pressing need for his business to grow. Money does not grow on trees after all, and it is important for the camp to keep one step ahead of the competition.

Farag's latest plan has been to rent the camp out to a new management team. He has found three fresh-faced graduates from Cairo who are keen to make their mark on the world and to put into practice the skills that they learnt on their Tourism degrees. The friends have a grand plan and are confident that within no time at all there will be coach-loads of tourists queuing to access the authentic Bedouin campfire experience that they will put on offer.

As well as the new restaurant, shop, and cybercafé, they have invested in a new Bedouin tent, with handwoven rugs and cushions surrounding the central campfire. This is where people spend their evenings now, sipping sweet tea from small glass cups, with their laughter echoed by the crackle of firewood and their smiling faces lit by the warm, orange glow.

Only a year and a half has passed since I was last here, but the camp is hardly recognisable. The *arisha* has gone and guests now dine in a modern restaurant, seated at smart wooden tables, cooled by electric ceiling fans. In front of the restaurant there is a new terraced seating area, perfect for drinking your morning coffee while enjoying the dappled shade provided from the newly planted vines and pink bougainvillea. This morning Kevin is hovering around the kitchen door, negotiating patiently with Iqbal, one of the new management team. Once he has secured the plate of food scraps needed to feed his feline friends he heads in my direction, sitting down at the bamboo table adjacent to mine.

"Olivia, welcome back," he says with a smile.

"It is great to see you again," I reply, happy to find that my old friend is still here despite all the changes.

"And I will be here until July, four whole months this time!" I continue, explaining to Kevin what drew me back here and introducing him to the four other students who are sitting by my side. I missed the mountains, of course, but there was also the economic recession which had made it hard for me to get a job. Instead of jumping into the competitive graduate job market, I had decided to continue my studies and had opted for a Master's degree which would allow me to spend months here in the mountain.

Iqbal is watching us as we speak, his slim frame leaning casually against the kitchen doorway. He has already fallen in love with the place. He was quick to absorb the tranquillity of the landscape and feels a sense of release, freed from the oppressive hustle and bustle of the Cairo backstreets. He is sure that they can make a success of this and is filled with a sense of quiet confidence and optimism as he looks out across the tourist-filled tables in front of him.

Iqbal spots the empty coffee cups collecting on our table and rushes to fill them, catching my eye and smiling on his way.

I have moved on from colour-changing lizards, deciding that there are more urgent issues that need researching. I was lucky enough to spend last summer in East Africa on a Tropical Biology Association field course where I saw first-hand how effectively and irreversibly we as humans are damaging our planet. The course was based in the Usambara mountains in Tanzania, where the remaining rainforests were brimming with life. The leaf litter crawled with over-sized millipedes and tiny frogs, delicate chameleons hung from the leaves, and troops of vocal monkeys swung amongst the canopies. Everywhere I looked, I was presented with something new. Sights, sounds and smells that stimulated all of my senses.

Despite this wealth of beauty, it was impossible to miss the fact that these forests were becoming increasingly isolated, surrounded on every side by vast stretches of tea plantations and farmland. The tea plantations were beautiful, swathes of vibrant green rolling towards the horizon, but they were void of forest life. When compared to the rich and vibrant sounds and sights of the forests that they replaced, they were nothing more than deserts. One evening, I watched a flock of hornbills flying across the tea fields, their unique forms silhouetted against the orange sky. They flew between the shrinking patches of forest, temporarily leaving themselves vulnerable and exposed. It was a breath-taking moment, both beautiful and unforgettable, but I could not relax until the birds had crossed the tea plantations and resubmerged themselves into the safety of their forest canopy.

After the course I travelled with my friend Beth across Tanzania, through Kenya and into Uganda, discovering extraordinary places and people along the way. We saw wildlife unlike any that we had encountered before, coming face to face with mountain gorillas in the forests of Bwindi, being chased by baboons in Queen Elizabeth National Park and dodging hippos in the dusky blue twilight of Lake Mburo. There were moments when I truly felt that we had discovered paradise. However, as we travelled between sites I could not help but notice the same pattern repeating itself. Every time we left the parks and moved out of the cities we drove through miles of farmland and plantations, where crops grew uniformly across lands that were once filled with life. I had known that modern agriculture was harming the environment, but now I really got it. Of course we need food to survive, but the way in which we are producing it is destroying our planet.

Farming is not inherently unsustainable. In the first few weeks of our travels, we visited a small homestead in the foothills of Mount Kilimanjaro. Our smiling tour guide, Ambrouse, showed us around his family village where the Chagga people still grow their crops in the traditional way. Here, there were multiple layers of flowering vegetables and yams, all flourishing beneath green bananas and coffee bushes, which in turn were nestled beneath a thinned canopy of forest trees. The children laughed, the birds sang and there was a mellow buzz of life. It was such a stark contrast to the monotonous tea plantations that I had worked in earlier that month. These Chagga people showed that it was possible to farm without destroying nature and they gave me hope.

Once I was back in the UK, I looked at the green fields and stretches of bright, yellow oil seed rape in a new way. Where I once saw light and colour, I now saw emptiness. On the surface things looked healthy, but I now understood that our farms were being propped up by fertilisers and pesticides.

Beneath it all, soils were crumbling, pollinators vanishing and hedgerows draining of life. It could not last.

Of course, the Bedouin knew how to do it properly. I kept thinking back to those high mountains, and the gardens that lay hidden amongst them, filled with fruits, nuts vegetables and herbs. There was so little rain, and the sun was so hot and heavy, but these orchard gardens had been kept alive for over one thousand years. I decided to spend my Master's learning how these gardens could be sustained amidst the expanse of rock and desert. I wanted to learn from that ancient wisdom and understand how the Bedouin were able to work with nature to keep their crops plentiful.

I didn't know it at the time, but I was starting a journey that would lead me deep into the mountains of St Katherine, where I would begin to uncover the secrets of those hidden gardens and the people that visited them.

## Chapter 4

This year I will be working with a new guide called Mansour, who will help me navigate the mountains and identify gardens to work in. I have been told that he speaks excellent English and has great knowledge of the local wildlife. Despite the praise, I am feeling nervous about meeting him. I am going to be spending the next four months working alone with this man and things will be a lot easier if I like him.

Farag Fox has arrange for Mansour to meet me here at the Camp for the first day of field work. I am sitting in the terraced restaurant area, walking boots on, rucksack packed, and scrutinising everyone who enters the camp. A rickety moped pulls up and in he comes, dressed in a worn, grey galabeya, the tribe's characteristic pale purple headscarf, and a pair of designer-esque wraparound sunglasses. He sits down near me, opening an old tin of tobacco and rolling a cigarette as a way of introducing himself. He lifts his sunglasses and reveals bright and intelligent eyes and I feel an immediate sense of relief. I think I will enjoy working with this guy.

Mansour is cool, but it is a calm and collected coolness that he might not even be aware of. Over the next few weeks, he helps me gain entry to dozens of gardens across the valleys, casually negotiating with the garden owners as if they are all old friends. Time after time we are invited to drink tea, always treated as honoured guests. A handwoven rug would be laid out in the shadiest spot, against a stone wall or beneath an orchard tree. Mansour would lie down and smoke, laughing and joking with the host as they crouch down and begin lighting the fire. The conversations are in Arabic, so I just sit back and relax, taking in the mountain views and watching as the black tea pot begins to bubble and boil on the open flames. The tea is always served in small glass cups, flavoured with fresh herbs or a handful of dried rose petals. The finishing touch is the heaped teaspoons of sugar, always stirred in at the end with a flourish

The whole process is filled with a sense of ritual and timelessness. After climbing for hours in the hot sun, the sweet tea and guaranteed welcome is a joy. However, there is only so much tea a person can drink. The nature of my work means that some days I visit up to five or six gardens and it is so difficult to say no to these generous offers of hospitality. I spend hours sipping sweet tea in the shade, when I should be working—I like to think of it as soaking up the local culture, rather than procrastinating.

When I do get the chance to work, I have two key objectives. Firstly, I have to collect soil samples with the hope of finding out how the soil quality and biodiversity differs between the gardens and the surrounding environment. At home, wide-scale use of pesticides and heavy machinery means that our soil is becoming compacted and void of life. This is a problem, as the hidden interactions between insects, worms, fungi, and bacteria are crucial for breaking down decaying matter, releasing nutrients and regenerating our soil. Without them, the only way to grow food is by adding artificial fertilisers, which themselves come at a cost. Here, the Bedouin avoid these chemicals and are able to create these productive and plentiful gardens using just a bit of goat manure and well-managed rainwater. I have a feeling that this success is helped by a healthy community of ground fauna, thriving in the wet, irrigated beds, and doing their bit by decomposing plant matter and allowing the next generation of crops to grow.

Secondly, I want to understand how the irrigation in the gardens is affecting the native plants and pollinators. I had noticed last year that the flowering vegetables and herbs within the gardens were alive with flashes of colourful butterfly wings and the hum of hoverflies and bees. However, outside on the dry mountain slopes, the plants were brown and desiccated. Some of them do produce a few flowers in a desperate attempt to reproduce, but I am worried that the bees will veer towards the flower-filled gardens, leaving these lonely plants to wither away unpollinated.

To find out what is going on I observe and record the pollinators that visit wild plants both inside and outside the gardens. In between my cups of tea I sit and stare at the delicate flowers of the unique mountain herbs, waiting for pollinators to visit and feed. Later in the season I will count the individual seeds produced by each flower, allowing me to test whether the isolated plants found on the high mountain sides are getting the same levels of pollination as those growing in the bountiful gardens down below. This involves me sitting quietly for hours in the hot mountain sun, scarf draped over my head and clipboard in hand, while Mansour reclines, gossiping and smoking, in the cool, deep shade of the gardens.

It requires patience. I often find my mind wandering, drifting across the valley slopes and up into the expansive blue sky, but the flutter of a wing or the buzz of a bee pulls me immediately back to the moment. The flower visits are few and far between, but there is exquisite variety, from velvety bees, metallic beetles, striped hoverflies, through to thin-waisted wasps. I would never usually choose to take the time to sit and stare, but it is a luxury. Even as days turn into weeks, there is always something new to see, a glimpse of a rare butterfly species or simply a quirk in the flight pattern of a particular bee.

Work continues back at camp, where I spend my afternoons sorting through the contents of the traps and typing up my notes from the day. Iqbal has let me use a corner of the restaurant as a makeshift lab, so a curious tourist may find me in my dusty field clothes, filtering through my trap contents, removing bits of rock and sand before extracting the grubby ants, ground beetles and springtails for preservation in ethanol. Today, the sun is beginning to set as I place the last springtail into its sample pot. I do not even open my laptop, but head straight to my room to wash before dinner.

The shower rejuvenates me, washing away the fatigue of the day and leaving a pool of brown grit on the floor in its wake. In my room, I stretch out on the hard mattress, feeling a satisfying release of tension in my muscles. Instead of resting, I start wondering how I am going to fill the evening. The days are busy and full, but when the sun drops and the temperature cools, I get filled with a restless energy, and the nights stretch out long and empty, begging to be filled.

I am sharing my room with Beth this year, and together we have found plenty of ways to fill our time. We have discovered the Plaza Hotel, the only retailer of alcohol in town, and regularly venture off into the night in search of overpriced rosé wine. Other nights we stick to the Bedouin tent, playing our music around the campfire, while smoking apple-flavoured tobacco from the camp's new sheesha pipe. My partner in crime is not here tonight, so after dinner I simply wander over to the Cybercafé to aimlessly check my emails.

Beth and another student, Amy, are both studying the ecology of the Sinai Baton Blue butterfly. This tiny blue-winged creature is smaller than your thumbnail and is rumoured to be the world's smallest butterfly. It is only found at high elevation, restricted by the range of its larval host plant, so Beth and Amy have to spend several nights each week camping amongst the mountain peaks. As I sit in the hot stuffy room, waiting for my emails to load on the outdated PC, they are probably eating rice around an open campfire and getting ready to curl up in their sleeping bags.

The hand-painted sign that describes this dusty room as a Cybercafé is somewhat misleading. The internet connection is intermittent and tediously slow, making it necessary to rock back and forth on the old wooden chairs while waiting for your website to load. I repeatedly check my emails, expecting nothing in particular. In the corner of the room, Iqbal is hanging out, chewing on small edible seeds, picking the edible centres from the salt-coated shells with his teeth.

"Ya Habibi," he says, throwing a shell at my back to get my attention.

"Kafa Halak? Colulo ta meme?" he follows, asking me how I am and if everything is well.

"Colulo quiess, wa anta?" I reply, appreciating the distraction.

I am beginning to understand the basics of the Arabic language, but I often automatically respond in English. I enjoy these evening chats with Iqbal. I feel relaxed enough to practice my Arabic without fear of judgement, knowing that if I mispronounce words he will just smile and laugh.

While Iqbal and I chat away, Kevin is sitting alone in his cave. He has been feeling increasingly low over the past few months, becoming distracted and anxious. He has started smoking with a deep ferocity, hoping that each inhalation will help lift him from the darkness. It never does, he thinks as he sits in the gloom, absentmindedly stroking the cats that pass across his lap. He is staring directly at a small blue light glowing from a ledge in the rock. It is an Mp3 player that had been given to him by a passing tourist last week. He is yet to press play, wary of the type of music that could be held in such a tiny machine.

Up above on the mountain top, Beth and Amy are preparing for bed. Their guide, Farhan, an old Bedouin man renowned for his multiple wives and poor cooking, cleans the pots and pans with bottled well-water that he collected earlier that day. He takes his cushioned mattress and a thick blanket and lays them out behind a boulder several metres from the girls. Beth also lies down, pulling her sleeping bag around her neck and breathing in the cool night air. She closes her tired eyes and feels her muscles relax against the cold rock beneath her mattress. The glowing embers of the campfire crackle and dim, leaving the now sleeping bodies wrapped in the blackness of the star-filled sky.

## *Chapter 5*

We have been here for two months now, and England feels a long way away. My boyfriend Pete is flying out to visit me tomorrow and I have booked a room for us in a tourist hotel by the sea. I know that I should be excited to share my new world with him, but I don't feel comfortable bringing him here to Fox Camp.

Instead of exploring the mountains and sleeping out under the stars, we spent the week in Dahab, drinking beers in the sunshine and snorkelling in the Red Sea. In a way it was perfect, but everything felt tinged with a sense of sadness. I longed for the shade of an orchard tree and a cup of tea by the fire. I missed the place I had begun to think of as home, and of course I missed the people.

Pete has gone home now, and I find myself sitting in my room staring at the first draft of a break-up text. I didn't have the guts to say it to his face. He had travelled over three thousand miles to see me and I could not bring myself to ruin the holiday.

I take a deep breath and press send. It is done. I crumple up into a ball, hit in the stomach by guilt and regret. I am a coward. You do not deserve this, Pete.

Work keeps me busy and after a couple of days digging up soil and staring at flowers I start to pull myself together. Life continues as normal in the camp, with long afternoons and evenings to fill. One of my new activities is to watch the cats. They offer a real-life soap opera, filled with drama, violence, and romance. Dinosaur, the rugged, black-coated male, can often be seen prowling around vulnerable young females and forcing them into unwanted sexual relations. On other days, Sophie, the camp's queen, will parade in front of him, tail high and thick coat gleaming. She will flaunt herself teasingly, a fine example of a cat who knows what she wants and how to get it.

"Taili henna," calls a voice from across the camp, distracting me from the cats. I look up and see Iqbal beckoning me to join him. I walk over to the office, where Tamir, one of the other camp managers, is holding two full plastic bags.

"A delivery from Dahab," explains Tamir as he places the bags down in front of us. We all crouch down and begin looking through the delivery, expecting practical items for the camp and some sweet treats for us. The bag contained some unexpected surprises. Tamir pulls out a box of teabags and gasps, his big brown eyes widening as he examines the image on the front of the box.

"What is this?" he asks.

"It is Tea for Men," I say, reading the aggressive black lettering on the top of the box.

"It is stamina-enhancing," I continue in a serious voice, holding back my laughter.

"And apparently it can keep you going all night...?" I finish, looking up questioningly at them both as they deny all knowledge of the purchase,

Iqbal reaches into the bag and pulls out a Love Potion, a dissolvable powder encased with the discreet imagery of embracing lovers. Next we find Energizer Tablets, covered in sexy red lips, followed by Muscle Maker pills and Love Machine coffee.

At that moment Farag Fox enters the office. He is a big man, dressed in military combat trousers and a camouflage jacket. He surveys the scene and immediately spots the boxes and jars scattered in front of us. Farag is furious. He says nothing, but swipes the products back into the bag and storms away, leaving the three of us giggling like naughty children who have stumbled into adult territory.

Gossip spreads like wildfire around here, so I make no assumptions about anyone's love life.

We begin to spend more time together after that. Quiet nights in the tent now end up with us dancing, the tinny beat of our Western music lifting Beth and me to our feet, with Iqbal and Tamir following. One evening our dance moves get so wild and free that part of the woven roof fabric gets knocked into the fire. The sudden heat pushes us back to the edges of the tent, and the intense orange flames leap upwards, coming dangerously close to the fabric roof. While I stand and stare, somebody in the background stays calm and douses the flames with a bucket of water. No real harm done, but the party is over.

Kevin avoids these loud evenings, preferring to visit the tent earlier in the day when things are calm. He disapproves of our antics and is not afraid of sharing his thoughts. When Francis, our project supervisor, visits for a week Kevin is quick to inform him about what is going on.

"Olivia and Beth have been smoking Sheesha pipes," he says angrily to Francis as we all sit eating lunch. Beth and I both freeze, embarrassed in front of our superior, but Francis just smiles and laughs.

"They are both adults, they can make their own decisions," he responds. Kevin stomps back to his cave, leaving me to relax and reflect upon the fact that Francis is a legend.

After a couple of hours sulking with his cats, Kevin emerges and joins us in the tent. A tourist has brought an old, battered viola with him and wants to know whether anyone in the camp can play. I look at Kevin, remembering the tales about his musical training in Israel, and the magic he could produce from an ocarina.

"You can play, can't you, Kevin?" I ask encouragingly. Kevin does not respond but eyes the case warily. After a few moments, he reaches out and opens the case, revealing the glossy curves of the stringed instrument inside. He lifts it tenderly, placing it underneath his chin and closing his eyes. Without saying a word, he picks up the bow and launches into a raft of classical melodies

Something opens up inside him. His fingers fly across the strings, recalling tunes from a life that had been left behind. The audience is transfixed, focused on Kevin, whose body moves with the power of the music as it carries away his pain. The instrument is not perfectly tuned, and Kevin has not touched a viola for years, but he plays the Mozart and Bach with such an earnest ferocity that I have to swallow back my tears. Here is a true musician.

When the spontaneous recital is over, we all stand and applaud.

Iqbal looks at me and says "*Helawa Sa*?" and I nod; it had been truly beautiful.

Kevin had not been playing for people's approval, though, and he smiles sheepishly in response to all the praise, shuffling out of the tent at the first opportunity.

Kevin did not know it at the time, but the music had reignited something within him. Over the next few weeks, he begins listening to the tracks on his new MP3 player, finding that certain tunes could sooth him, others could energise him, and one or two could lift him skywards towards the moon. He felt more in control of things now that he could readjust his mood with the press of a button. It was time to look ahead to the future. His parents had sent him money to buy a flight home to England, but perhaps he could use the money to fly to Peru instead. He could almost taste the sacred Iowasca that he would soon sip beneath the rustling canopy of rainforest trees.

He does not get around to buying the flights but, by the end of the year, he feels ready to say goodbye to Fox Camp. He packs his few belongings, kisses Sophie and the remaining cats farewell and gets a taxi to the coast. From there, he travels across the sea to Jordan and begins to build a new life. He rents a small space and hosts an art exhibition, showing the public old, sepia photographs of St Katherine Monastery and the mountains that he loves.

There is about to be a similar shift in my life. Beth is up in the mountains tonight, so I have our room to myself. There is a gentle knock at the door. I open it to find Iqbal, looking nervous and excited.

"Ya Habibi, will you come with me?" Iqbal whispers, stretching out his hand in the darkness.

I take it trustingly and follow him. We tip-toe down the lamp-lit path between the bedrooms and the olive grove and then he leads me up a narrow staircase, along the backs of the rooms and towards the top of the restaurant roof. There is a steep and rocky path and we stumble as we climb, stifling our laughter in the darkness.

When we make it, the night is silent. The moon has yet to rise, and the stars flicker brightly above us. We take a moment to gaze upwards, where the Milky Way spirals infinitely into the darkness. Then our shoulders touch, our hands meet and the magic happens.

In the early hours of the morning, we lie together in the heat, my tanned arm draped across his pale, delicate chest. I look at the contrast in our skin tones. I have only ever seen his brown face and arms, but the rest of his body is untouched by the sun.

"Your skin is so pale!" I say as I gently kiss the soft skin of his chest. I love being alone with him. We are different people in here. Free from the preconceptions and judgements that hang over us in the outside world.

We spend every night together after that. When Beth is here, we move from room to room, hoping each night that there will be one that is unoccupied by tourists. Wherever we are, those four walls provide security, giving us the space to explore the secrets of each other's bodies and learn the intimacies of each other's minds.

We talk late into the night, cocooned in the shabby room of choice, on the thin mattress with cheap, brightly coloured sheets. We share memories of our childhoods, drifting between the green hills of Somerset and the banks of the Nile. Iqbal talks of his little sister who dreams of training as a doctor, me of my brother who has had the chance to do so. I talk of the cows that could be seen from my bedroom window, he of the first-hand reality of growing up on a working farm.

One story that makes me smile is that of Iqbal and the baby goat. When he was a boy, he begged his father to let him rescue a tiny goat that he saw abandoned by the side of the road. Back at home, he provided the kid with round the clock care, attending to its every need, stroking its delicate grey fur as he bottle-fed it night and day. The kid was soon up and about, exploring the outside world, where one day the hot mid-summer sun was too much. Iqbal found the limp, sweaty creature unconscious on the hot stone floor and knew exactly what to do. He whipped up the kid and rushed to the bathroom shower. Iqbal crouched with the animal in his arms for over an hour, cold water pouring over the two of them. Once its body temperature had cooled, the kid came round, opening its eyes and bleating. I love the image of this kind, young boy sitting with the wet kid in his arms. I feel proud of him. Iqbal had saved the goat's life.

Sometimes Iqbal rests his face against my stomach, gazing up at me and asking, "Habibi, will you let us make a baby?"

I always laugh and tell him I am far too young.

Occasionally, though, I see something in the smooth curve of his neck that reminds me of my brother as a small boy. I think of those happy summers spent with my brother playing together in our garden and, for a moment, I imagine Iqbal and me creating our own child. I think of its soft, pretty neck and how it would be loved and adored. Even more than that little goat.

A girl can dream.

# 2011

*Olivia with Bedouin
garden in background*

# Chapter 6

It is early summer, and the temperature is rising. Down by the coast, the sun hangs heavily in the clear sky and the black tarmac roads glint with the heat. Despite the weather, Carlos is embarking on a journey. He is armed with nothing but the clothes on his back and the flip-flops on his feet. He is determined to walk all the way to St Katherine. It starts off well and the old man covers the first twenty miles easily, fuelled by a sense of destiny. He is on a pilgrimage, or a fated quest to reach the holy land of Mount Sinai and nothing is going to stop him.

The hours pass by, and Carlos continues onward. Around him there is nothing except an expanse of rocky desert and the occasional passing camel. The road that he is following stretches out for miles before disappearing into a glimmering haze at the horizon. He must admit that his excitement is waning. The plastic of his cheap flip-flops is beginning to blister his toes, and it is ever so hot.

By the time the sun reaches its peak, he is really being tested. The heat is oppressive, and he needs water. His mouth is dry, grating like sandpaper, while his shirt is saturated and dripping with sweat. His scalp is burnt now, red and peeling, and his thoughts are becoming unfocused. He feels increasingly dizzy.

Human kindness will be Carlos's salvation. When he is at his worst, a white Toyota pick-up speeds towards him. The young driver spots the penniless Peruvian man wilting by the

side of the road and grinds to a halt without hesitation. The driver passes him a cool bottle of water through the window, and after a swift exchange, Carlos finds himself lying in the back of the truck, wind in his face, and being given a free lift to the sacred Monastery of St Katherine.

My own journey to St Katherine went more smoothly. It is late evening by the time my taxi emerges from the star-kissed mountains into the town. The main road is now lit by rows of bright streetlights that illuminate the way into the camp. I am travelling alone this year, visiting Beth who has decided to continue her research and is now studying for a PhD. I am welcomed with a big hug from my friend, who is looking healthy and tanned. Within minutes of my arrival, I am being served sweet tea by the fire. It feels like coming home.

Everything feels so familiar, but someone is missing. Farag Fox has said goodbye to the young management team, sending Iqbal and his friends back to Cairo unemployed and in search of work. Instead, the camp is back under Farag's control, with a new manager, chef, and room keeper, called Hamza.

My first real encounter with Hamza comes later that week. Beth is working up in the mountains, giving me the time and space to reflect. I have climbed up onto the restaurant roof, retracing the steps that I once took with Iqbal. I miss him. We spoke on the phone for a while, and it was painful being apart. The last time I heard from him he shared a photograph of himself sitting amongst the protests in Tahir Square. He was with friends, looking relaxed and wearing my black and grey striped jumper. For a moment I felt as if I was there with him, amidst the chaos of the revolution.

Today, I feel alone, sitting on the roof in the late afternoon sun without him. I close my eyes and remember our last night here. It was our farewell party. We were all up here eating and drinking. Iqbal lay in my arms. Beth and Tamir laughed by my side, and up above the bats piped in the starlit sky.

"You miss him, habibi," says Hamza who has silently appeared at my side.

I jump, quickly wiping the tears from my eyes.

"This is for you," he continues, placing a cheap metal ring in my palm.

I feel unnerved. How does this man know about me and Iqbal? How does he know this is our special place?

"Take one, yaini, it will make you feel good," he follows, offering me a cigarette.

I do not usually smoke, but I accept the cigarette anyway. I inhale deeply, hoping it will help me tolerate the chatter of this strange and unnerving man.

Hamza has a habit of observing everybody who enters the camp in minute detail. He is *Sa'idi*, coming from Upper Egypt, so is considered an outsider by the local Bedouin who live here. It is part of his job to provide Bedouin visitors with a continual supply of tea and it makes him furious to get dumped with all the work but none of the social benefits. Hamza much prefers serving the tourists, particularly the women, who get his full attention whenever they are present in camp.

Evenings in the camp are different with Hamza here. He takes every opportunity to invite young women and their partners to the tent, where they will be bombarded by his banter and apparent charm. They are serenaded by the sound of the *Sa'idi* beat played enthusiastically on the tabla drum, and invited to clap, sing, or even dance with him to the hypnotic beat. Hamza is particularly proud of his hip-rolling dance moves and happily takes centre-stage, gyrating confidently for the clapping tourists. He rarely thinks of the wife and child who he has left behind. Life is for the living after all.

On quieter nights Hamza can still be found in the tent by the fire. Once he is sure that the boss has gone home and the secret police are out of sight, he can whip out his stash from beneath the cushions and rolls himself a well-deserved joint. Sometimes he is joined by relaxed tourists and young men from the village, such as Qasim and Kamal. On these nights, laughter drifts out of the tent into the darkness and all seems right in the world. But tonight, the tourists are all asleep and Hamza's so-called friends have disappeared early, leaving him smoking alone in the darkness.

Hamza struggles with sleep, often staying awake until the early hours. This morning, in the pale blue dawn, he lies by the dying embers of the fire, half asleep but still conscious of every movement in the camp. While he tosses and turns, our weary traveller Carlos is enjoying a deep and restorative sleep in the monastery guest house down the road. When the golden sunlight begins streaming through his bedroom window, Carlos awakes feeling rejuvenated and ready for the last stage of his journey.

Carlos knows that it is his calling to follow in the footsteps of Moses and reach the summit of Mount Sinai. Yes, officially visitors are required to hire a local Bedouin guide when climbing these mountains, but Carlos is confident that he can do this alone. Face washed and flip flops on, he sets off with a skip in his step. He avoids the well-trodden tourist trails and instead is guided by pure instinct.

He is drawn towards the narrow gullies and the curious crevices, laughing at the thrill of leaping from rock to rock. His mind has never been so alive but his old body is struggling to keep up. His calves shake and his blistered feet slip and fail to keep their grip. Carlos falls. The world turns in slow motion. He is aware of the thudding of his limbs against rock, the shattering of his gold watch-face, the crack of his skull. And then, silence.

Carlos's body lies crumpled at the base of a deep gulley. In the distance, crowds of tourists climb the ancient trails, safely reaching the mountain summit unaware of the horror that lies hidden below them. The fall had ended with the collision of skull against stone, leaving Carlos unconscious and bleeding, with little chance of being found.

It is rare for people to leave the established trails but on this particular day, Joao, a new Master's student, is out exploring the mountains, scanning the cracks and crevices with his binoculars. He is searching for the white-crowned wheatear, a small black and white bird that places intriguing piles of rocks in front of its nest. Known locally as the *Bhagar*, these characteristic birds are thought to be bringers of luck. It is the glint of the gold wristwatch that catches Joao's eye, drawing his attention to the collapsed old man. Joao moves with speed and agility, confidently navigating his way down to Carlos's side. He uses his scarf to apply pressure to the head wound and then tries phoning for help.

There is no phone signal, but Joao does not panic. Using the rush of adrenaline to climb back up the rocks, he moves between the boulders in search of a signal. He holds his phone high in the air and then finds it, one bar, enough to call for help. After making the call, Joao returns to sit beside the unconscious man, resting his hand on Carlos's shoulder and waiting patiently for assistance to arrive.

Help comes, and Carlos is carried down the mountain and immediately transported to the hospital in Sharm El Sheikh. The problem is, he carried nothing with him, and without money or a passport, he is unable to pay the bill. Farag Fox comes to the rescue, covering all of the costs with the condition that Carlos would come and work at the camp until the debt was settled.

And so it is that our paths cross and I find myself being served hummus and sheesh kebabs by this smiling Peruvian man. When I have finished eating, Carlos joins me for tea. His head is bandaged, and he is wearing ill-fitting, borrowed clothes, but he talks enthusiastically and is full of energy. He begins with stories of his life in Peru. I hear about his daughter who does not speak to him and his wife who does not care.

"You see, that is why I had to journey here to this holy land," he says emphatically. "It was my calling, a mission from God," he continues, speaking with passion and conviction. "Put your life in God's hands. It gives you freedom. Up in the mountains there is no responsibility. Jump one way, and you may break an arm. Jump the other you break your neck. But it is God's choice. You are free."

I nod along, sipping at my tea.

"You should try it!" he concludes, meeting my eye with genuine sincerity.

"It sounds dangerous. I think I will stick to the paths," I reply gently.

I know the story's ending and choose to put my trust in the ancient trails rather than the ancient gods.

Carlos goes on to enjoy many months working in Fox Camp, chatting with tourists and sharing stories about the exhilaration of placing your fate in God's hands. He feels safe there, but eventually the time comes for him to move on. Once his debts are paid, he heads off to Cairo in search of a route home. Things do not go well in the big, busy capital city and he soon finds himself face to face with armed police, being accused of petty theft. Without cash to pay a bribe and with no identification documents, Carlos is arrested and locked up in one of the city's largest prisons.

He shares a hot and crowded cell with other inmates, guilty of unknowable crimes. It is sweltering, the air thick with sweat and the buzz of biting insects. Arabic shouts reverberate between the concrete walls, thwarting Carlos's attempts to share the tales of his adventures. Eventually he gives up, turning inwards and blocking out their sound.

Six months later, he is released. He is worn and thin, and wanders the streets feeling lost, until a kind stranger directs him to the Embassy. Before long they have arranged for him to be put on a flight back home. It should have been a happy ending, but as that plane set off from Cairo to Lima the cabin air pressure began to drop, triggering a brain haemorrhage that damaged his optic nerve. Carlos finds himself in hospital once again, before finally making it back to his small, empty house where he sits and reflects upon the year. There had been ups and downs. It was going to be difficult living life as a blind man but he would adapt. The thing that really bugs him, is that he never did make it to the summit of Mount Sinai. His journey was never finished. Perhaps he should try again next year.

# *Chapter 7*

The two weeks in Sinai flew by and before I know it, I am back in Bristol. I am now working as a research assistant on the Urban Pollinator Project at the University, spending my days surveying pollinators across the city streets. We often get bemused looks from passers-by, a strange trio of scientists armed with clipboards, insect nets and specimen jars. It is great fun. We laugh and we learn, and I start to notice bees and hoverflies everywhere I go.

It is a short-term contract, and I have been busy applying for PhDs on the side. I have had interviews in Cambridge, Leeds, and York, but none of them successful and none of them quite right. I miss the mountains. I go on to write a grant application to try and get back out there, but once again face rejection.

It is all starting to feel like an impossibility but then I receive the email I have been waiting for. Francis has won a large Leverhulme grant to continue our work on the biodiversity and ecosystem services within the Bedouin gardens.

And he is offering me a PhD! I accept without hesitation and move back up to Nottingham to reconnect with my old life.

By April 2012, I am heading back out to Sinai with Beth, who is now in the final year of her PhD, and three new Master's students, Sean, Lisa and Luke. This year I am going to use the skills I learnt in Bristol and assess how plant-pollinator interactions differ between the gardens and the surrounding landscape.

First things first: we need to decide which guides to work with. This has never been a problem in the past—we have all happily employed the guide recommended to us by Farag. But now Beth and I have insider knowledge and we both agree that the best guide in town is the one and only Mansour.

Last year Beth and Mansour spent months working together up on the mountain. Beth worked solidly during the days and Mansour learnt to read her every need. He fed her biscuits when her sugar levels dropped, gave her tea when she began to flag and cracked jokes when her mood dropped too low. In the evenings they laughed together beside the fire, and at night they slept within a stone's throw of one another, close enough to hear each other breathing.

For me, Mansour has amazing knowledge of the gardens and connections with the garden owners. He understands the intricacies of my work and, if I am honest, I do not think I can do it without him.

"You should work with Mansour" Beth says, reading my mind.

"Really? Are you sure?" I reply, with excitement creeping into my voice.

She nods and I accept gratefully. Perhaps I should have argued, insisted that she work with someone she knows and trusts up there on the mountain, but I don't. I just give her a massive hug and thank her for being such a wonderful and kind friend.

Thanks to Beth, Mansour and I are soon back at work in the gardens. This year I have decided to extend my surveys, stretching from down here in the town up into the high mountains. All of these gardens belong either to the monastery or to the local tribe, the Gebeliya. The Gebeliya have an ancient connection with St Katherines, and some say that they are descendants of Wallachian workers brought here over one thousand years ago to build the monastery. Many of the Gebeliya still work within the monastery gardens, tending to the rows of olive trees that produce oil for the monastery lamps. The rest of the tribe have adopted the farming practices that were brought here from Europe, building stone walls, dams and terracing to capture the rainwater that pours through the valleys after the intermittent flash floods. Over the generations, these Byzantine practices have been adapted and moulded into the landscape, creating the unique fruit-filled gardens that are here today.

In English, the term Gebeliya translates into the "mountain people", and as such their tribal range covers all these mountains. There are another ten tribes found across the Peninsular, each occupying a distinct range. I am becoming familiar with the neighbouring tribes, the Garasha, who roam the southern deserts below here, and the Muzeina tribe whose range stretches out along the eastern coast.

Each tribe has a unique culture and heritage. The Gebeliya's relationship with the monks and the cooler climate of the mountains means that they are the only tribe with a history of farming, while the Garasha depend on grazing and the Muzeina on fish. Most of the Garasha were nomadic, moving across the desert with their herds, but a few families settled in desert oases which have become tall, impressive palm groves.

These desert groves have many similarities with the mountain gardens, but their stone walls contain heat-tolerant date palms instead of the blossoming apricots, apples, pears, and pomegranates that are found at higher elevations. From what I have seen through the taxi window, the lowland desert that surrounds them consists of miles of dusty scrub, interspersed by the odd acacia tree. Real isolation.

Yes, the mountain gardens also appear isolated at first glance, but the rocky cracks and crevices hide lizards, nesting wheatears, and delicate medicinal herbs. I cannot imagine such life in the flat lowlands, where temperatures soar ten degrees centigrade higher than on the mountain peaks.

I suspect that the desert palm groves will have a very different value for local wildlife. Perhaps they will also be filled with bees and butterflies, but maybe not, as the palms do not flower like the orchard trees, and the landscape could simply be too empty to support such life. I have no choice but to include them in my study to find out.

In other words, it is time for a road trip.

Qasim pulls into camp in his familiar Land Cruiser that has the letters F.O.X. painted on the side in large blue script. He checks out his reflection in the mirror, rearranging his headscarf before strolling towards us. He is dressed immaculately, in a crisp white galabeya, a blingy gold watch, and dark sunglasses. He moves towards us with a confident elegance, then flashes us the bright smile of a celebrity.

I am sitting with Beth and Mansour, who are both joining me for the ride. Mansour jumps up and welcomes Qasim with the hug of old friends. Qasim will be driving us to the low desert, to the oasis of Ain Hodra and the palm groves of Wadi Fieran. Over two days I will carry out my plant and pollinator surveys and at night we will camp in the desert, where Mansour is planning on cooking up a feast.

We all pile into the Land Cruiser with excitement, the two men in the front and Beth and me sitting opposite each other in the back. Without saying a word, Qasim turns the music up, lights a cigarette, places his foot on the accelerator and we are off.

At first we stick to the main road, but after passing through the checkpoints Qasim swerves off to the left, leading us directly into the desert. The car bumps across the uneven track and I feel an unexpected sense of freedom. We are surrounded by a vast emptiness, which stretches out in all directions. Qasim drives casually, one hand on the wheel, his other elbow resting on the windowsill, and navigates the rocky landscape with ease.

The terrain begins to alter, white sand replacing the rocky earth. Then out of nowhere, we hit a ravine, sheer cliffs descending down in front of us. Beth and I fall silent and Qasim turns around and grins.

He drives up on to a hidden track, not much wider than the car itself. We move slowly, Qasim handling the drops and turns one by one with careful consideration. I look out of the window behind me and feel my stomach turn. There is nothing, we are teetering on the edge of an abyss. To make things worse, the path tilts angling the Land Cruiser directly over the chasm. I let out a nervous squeak and together Beth and I start to giggle, our laughter both filled with exhilaration and tinged with fear.

We make it across unscathed. Qasim is a pro; he has used this route to impress tourists countless times and it certainly works. The view of Ain Hodra is now opening up in front of us, the green colours of the oasis shimmering on the horizon. I feel like Lawrence of Arabia, albeit with a Land Cruiser rather than a camel.

As we approach, the oasis begins to take shape, dry stone walls and barbed wire enclosing the tall palms that stretch up high above us. We drive in through a painted metal gate and park up beneath the shade of a tree. It is hot down here. I look around. The oasis is split into individually owned gardens, each filled with date palms and not much else. There is more space here, trees spread far apart with dusty earth beneath them. I spot a few beds of flowering herbs and alfalfa for the goats, but on the whole there seems to be less for the pollinators. I set to work, Mansour and Qasim chatting in the shade, Beth helping me measure out my survey areas and keeping me company as I identify the plants and net any insects that I see visiting the flowers.

After a few hours surveying the gardens within the oasis, Beth and I head outside down into a wide valley of soft white sand. We repeat the surveys out here, finding even less, just the occasional wild herb. The surveys are much quicker than they are in the mountains, but the heat is exhausting. When we get back, we find that the rain-fed pool in the centre of the oasis has been filled with cans of Coke. It feels like a godsend.

The four of us sit with our feet dangling in the cool water, fishing out the ice-cold cans and imbibing the sweet liquid. It has been a long day's work and the sun soon starts to set, the sky turning a hazy, purplish blue.

The hum of mosquitoes emerges around us. The oasis is full of them. They are bigger and louder than those in found in Fox Camp and more aggressive. I start swiping around, smacking the little creatures as they bite at my face and neck.

We are not camping here, so now is the time to move on. Qasim drives us deeper into the desert, away from the water and the breeding ground of the biting insects. As we pass through the wide valley it begins to open out, rocky cliffs being replaced by rolling sand dunes. When we stop, it feels like pure isolation, nothing but sand and sky and the small crescent moon.

The sky is beginning to darken as we pull the mattresses out from the back of the car. We need wood for our fire but looking around us there is nothing. In the mountains Mansour finds dry twigs and plant stems with ease, hardly needing to move from where he has crouched, but here he sets off as though it is a mission, inviting Beth to join him. The two of them set off towards the horizon, disappearing behind a rolling sand dune, leaving Qasim and me alone together.

I have known Qasim for several years now and he has always captured my attention. I remember the first time I met him in a garden at the base of Wadi Shraig and will not forget the evening we spent together in Dahab by the lagoon. I had been there waiting to see Iqbal again when Qasim arrived out of the blue with a young friend of ours who had never left the village. The teenage boy had never seen the sea and danced in the silver water as we sipped beer in the fading evening light.

We have also spent many evenings together in the tent, Qasim playing the guitar with us all clapping and laughing. But he is hard to pin down. His presence often kickstarts the party, but then he vanishes leaving Hamza and the rest of us at a loss.

This is the first time we have been alone together. Just Qasim and me. We walk together, picking up the odd twig for the fire before sitting and waiting for the others to return. We say little, but Qasim reaches out and places his hand gently upon mine. It is a delicate gesture. I gaze at his long, beautiful fingers before looking up, our eyes locking. We are alone in a desert in the near darkness. I could feel threatened right now but I don't. His gesture feels like a question that opens up new possibilities and I smile.

"We're back!" calls Beth in a sing song voice, interrupting the moment. The two of them emerge from behind the dune, Mansour grinning and carrying half a tree on his back. The dried branches are soon hacked into pieces, the fire is roaring and a secret bottle of red wine is being passed round in small glass cups.

It is party time.

## Chapter 8

It was a fantastic night. We dined upon fire-roasted goat beneath the twinkling stars. The flickering flames lit our laughing faces and the warm glow seemed to connect us. Four friends shielded from the darkness beyond.

The following day we arrive back at camp tired but happy, our hair and clothes filled with sand. Beth and I say little about our trip, instead holding on to it like a shared secret. Life carries on as normal. Beth spends several nights a week up in the mountain with her new guide Abdul, who Farag identified as a young man in need of employment. Abdul has three young children who he is struggling to feed, and he knows the mountains like the back of his hand. He is doing the job but he is quiet, with a fierce and intense glare that unnerves me.

Like Beth, Sean is also studying the ecology of a rare and endemic butterfly and spends most nights camping in the mountains. The Sinai Hairstreak butterfly inhabits inaccessible wadis that are off the tourist trail, so Sean spends his days scrambling up and down valleys near to Jebel Bab el Donya. I have always wanted to go there but people have warned me about the toughness of the climb. The mountain's name holds a certain magic, "the door to the world", with views extending across the entire mountain range down to the glimmering coastline at the edge of it all.

Like me, Luke and Lisa are both based at camp. Luke is continuing research into the nesting behaviour of the luck-bringing *Bhagar*, the bird that Joao was searching for on the day of Carlos's fall. This bird, the white crowned wheatear, places a collection of rocks in front of the crevice in which it nests, creating a rattling runway of precarious stones, which he thinks may provide a warning signal for nesting birds. If a snake tries to approach the nest it will disturb the rocks and the sound will alert the female so that she can fly back and protect her eggs.

Lisa's work is on a different scale and involves using motion-sensitive camera traps to survey wolf and hyena populations across the entire St Katherine region. Lisa is obsessed with wolves. When she talks about them her voice becomes fast and fiery, and she waves her arms in a passionate, Italian way. I have been coming here for years now, sleeping peacefully and unprotected beneath the stars with no idea that there could be wolves lurking in the darkness. I had known about the snow leopards that had been hunted to extinction and seen the leopard trap, made of great stone slabs which remains near Wadi Gebel, and I had just presumed that other carnivores had shared the same fate.

Luckily, Lisa suspects that both the wolves and hyena stick to the lower desert rather than the high mountains, so I do not need to worry. They are rarely seen, and little is known about their actual distribution. It is Lisa's mission to find out more.

I went with her one night earlier this month. We climbed a small mountain in the midst of the desert where she played pre-recorded wolf calls into the moonlit sky, hoping that a nearby pack would respond to the sound of an unknown call in their territory. We did not get a response, but simply standing there in the silvery light, listening to the recording of their howls gave me a deep respect for the animal.

Although as a group we are undertaking so much fascinating research, when in camp we tend to switch off. We stop being scientists and instead chat nonsense with Hamza or gossip about the cats. Luke enjoys crashing out in front of repeated episodes of Futurama on his laptop, while Lisa prefers sunbathing, hanging a blanket above the entrance to our bedrooms to keep away prying eyes. Sean retains some semblance of an ecologist, often wandering through the garden in search of rare birds.

Night-time is when I come alive. I gravitate towards the tent, attracted like a moth to the glow of the flames, never knowing quite who I will meet or what will happen. Some nights it is eerily quiet, everyone sleeping apart from Hamza who smokes alone in the office. Other nights it is filled with noisy, excited tourists preparing to climb the mountain when it is best to retreat to my room. But more often than not, I come across visiting tourists who share stories of their lives, or Gebeliya from the village, some of whom stare unpleasantly, others who are becoming good friends.

Tonight is cool and gentle, with quiet chattering and sipping of mint tea by the fire. The atmosphere is one of tired contentment and I head off to my room happy to have an early night.

Oh, but I must not forget to tell you the news. Sophie is pregnant. And odds are that Dinosaur is the father.

It is 2a.m. when my phone rings. I peer at the screen and see that it is Beth, ringing from her room on the other side of camp.

"I have been stung!" she squeals. "By a scorpion. On my bottom!" she finishes as I get to my feet.

"I am coming," I say as I start running across camp in my pyjamas. Beth is standing at her bedroom door, her face pursed with pain.

"It's still there," she says, pointing to a scorpion lying silently on the mattress.

I know that the toxicity of scorpion venom varies amongst species and that here in Sinai there is one that has the potential to kill.

"I will take a photo – so we know which species it is." I say, snapping the creature with my phone.

"And the next step is to kill it," I say confidently as I look around the room for a weapon. I opt for a flip-flop and whack the scorpion with all my might.

It was a spur of the moment thing. Retrospectively, a flip-flop was not the best choice as the bendy plastic simply pressed the scorpion into the squashy mattress. When I lifted it, the uninjured scorpion immediately ran away, disappearing down the side of the bed. Beth lets out a small laugh, which turns into a whimper as she feels the pulsating pain spread across her backside.

I run next door and bang on Sean's door. He has the identification guide and he will definitely know what species it was. Sean opens the door with ruffled hair and sleep in his eyes but as soon as he hears what has happened he jumps into action. He flips through the pages of the book, looking intently at the shape of the tail and pincers in the small photograph.

Outside, Hamza has heard the commotion and is talking to Beth, asking where the scorpion has gone. He starts searching beneath the bed and in the grubby corners of the room, determined to find and kill it.

Beth sits on the wall opposite her room, shivering now, her face turning pale. I join her and put my arm around her, hoping that everything will be okay.

At this point, Luke emerges and sees Hamza searching Beth's room.

"Hamza!" he calls. "My room is filled with mosquitoes."

Hamza ignores him, lifting up the mattress and propping it against the wall.

Luke continues undeterred. "Can you do something about it? It is a nightmare."

I shake my head and pull my arm tighter around Beth's shoulder. Sean rushes out, his finger pointing at a picture in the book. He has successfully identified the scorpion.

It is the Deathstalker.

Beth and I move to the office, while Hamza and Sean search her room and Luke grumbles about the mosquitoes. Beth curls up on the armchair and I open my laptop to login to the office Wi-fi and begin some research.

I start with the Wikipedia page which describes the species in detail:

*The deathstalker is one of the most dangerous species of scorpion. Its venom is a powerful mixture of neurotoxins, with a low lethal dose.*

*While a sting from this scorpion is extraordinarily painful, it normally would not kill a healthy adult human.*

"Hmm," I mumble as I process the information, deciding which bits to share. "Well, on the positive side, it rarely kills a healthy adult, so try not to worry," I say, smiling encouragingly.

I continue my research. There is an anti-venom vaccine, but from what I can tell it tends to be used in emergencies only. I think of the hospital, which is less than a mile from camp. It is reassuring to know that it is there but I do not trust it.

I am wary of seeking medical help here. I think back to the time when I was sick. I had severe diarrhoea and vomiting and the doctor was called from the village. He rocked up in a leather jacket and hooked me up to a drip, tying it to the mosquito net that hung above me. He left the discarded needle and its wrapping on the bathroom floor, along with a scattering of pills. He had missed my vein so the fluid pumped into my soft-tissues, inflating my arm into a heavy, sausage-like balloon. Beth saw the funny side and took lots of photos, but it is not something I would rush to repeat.

Best to keep Beth here if we can. I will just stay right beside her, watch her closely and check that she is okay. If things get bad, we can jump in a car and be at the hospital within minutes.

Hamza comes in and hands Beth a large mug of tea. She sips at it gratefully, enjoying the sweetness, unaware of the opium that he has mixed within it. The opiates take effect nonetheless. She begins to feel a loosening in her cramping limbs, a slowing of her pounding heart, and release from the throbbing pain in her head.

When Beth finishes the drink Hamza reveals what he has done. She is furious that he has gone behind her back and spiked her drink. But she cannot hide her relief at the reduction in pain. Hamza takes her anger in his stride and proceeds to press play on a YouTube video, a wide grin on his face. It is Enrique Inglesias singing "I will be your hero baby, I will kiss away your pain." It is hard to remain angry. Beth laughs and together we sing along, replaying the video time after time until the early hours of the morning.

Beth sleeps in my room that night so that I can keep an eye on her. She tosses and turns, groaning from the pain. By the morning the symptoms are easing. She spends the next day in bed, her strength returning, although her head remains fuzzy and her thoughts dampened. By the following morning she is up and about, and I am delighted. She is alive. She has survived the Deathstalker.

Survival is not enough though, because today we have all made plans to climb the highest mountain in Egypt, Gabal Katrine or Mount Katherine. I suggest that Beth could stay here and rest or we could rearrange the trip for another week, but she is determined to climb.

We set off early that afternoon, the five students, Beth included, with Mansour leading the way. The plan is to climb to the base of the mountain where we will spend the night, rising early the next morning to reach the summit and watch the sunrise. The climb isn't easy and takes nearly five hours. The sky darkening by the time we get near our base camp. The route leads us through the familiar, tree-lined Wadi Arbien, and then up and over into less familiar valleys. As we continue upwards the gardens become fewer and the distinctive peak of Gabal Katrine has disappeared from the horizon, instead becoming the rock beneath our feet.

Up here the familiar red granite and flowering herbs are replaced by stretches of bleak grey rock. The climb is steep and incessant, making Beth's weakened muscles shudder and shake. But she says nothing. She just clenches her jaw and pushes through her pain.

I drop back to walk with her. We are nearly there, a final push before we reach the camp. Up ahead, our friends have become silhouetted, black against the fading sky. On a distant cliff edge stands a lonely donkey, watching our forms slowly complete the day's final ascent.

The sky is thickening with cloud when we settle down for the night. Our campsite is exposed, with the dark grey of the peak looming behind us. The group is tired so after eating we try to sleep. Sean struggles, waking regularly in the night to hear mice scurrying across his sleeping bag, unaware that a bag of peanuts has been left at his feet.

Beth also struggles to sleep. Not because of her symptoms but because she is acutely aware of the presence of Mansour lying beside her.

We wake before dawn and scramble to the summit. The night is black and cold, the stars hidden by cloud. We huddle against the rock until the sun creeps upon us, shifting the clouds from grey through to white. It is as if we are floating, the world below us masked beneath the haze. But it does not compare to the last time I came here, and I feel like I have brought everyone here on false pretences.

Then, we had climbed through the night, sitting up here beside the chapel, bathed in moonlight. We had watched the round moon roll through the sky as the sun emerged to replace it. I saw the world split in two, the east cast in a golden light while the west remained in darkness.

For one beautiful moment, the two glimmering spheres had become perfectly aligned in the sky.

And time stood still.

# Chapter 9

We have been invited to a wedding.

No, we do not actually know the couple, but our young friend who danced in the sea has asked us to come to the wedding of his elder brother. We have no idea what to expect, but of course we say yes.

Beth, Lisa, and I dress up in our finest, long maxi dresses, with cardigans and scarves to keep things modest. Sean and Luke simply wear their smartest shirts and walking trousers. When we arrive, Sean and Luke are directed outside, while Beth, Lisa and I are taken into a large room, filled with women and children.

I have met very few female Bedouin and feel a bit overwhelmed by the dozens of women dressed entirely in black. Out in the gardens, I do occasionally come across women and children, but I tend to be invited to sit with Mansour and the men. Women often serve me tea, their faces covered by their scarves, and though I thank them it is too easy to overlook them, their facelessness making them dissolve into the background.

The other barrier is language. The men here interact regularly with tourists so speak basic English, but the women are restricted to their homes. When I am invited into the women's quarters they bombard me with questions, outwitting me with their fast-paced Arabic, leaving me embarrassed and confused. When I fail to respond, the questions are repeated, loud and insistent, making me shrink back against the wall and wish I was outside with the men. It is shameful, and I promise to sign up for Arabic lessons when I get home.

We hover for a while, before being ushered to take a seat on the floor. People keep drifting in until the decision is made to shut the door, signalling change. The women whip off their black outer garments, revealing a rainbow of colours below. Reds, golds, yellows, and blues, some modest, others skin-tight and encrusted with sequins.

Guests are first served hibiscus tea in plastic cups, bright pink and packed with sugar. Young girls watch curiously as we drink, smiling coyly if any of us catch their eye. Next come large circular platters brimming with steaming rice and slow-roasted goat, which are placed down on the floor in front of the sitting groups of women. There is no cutlery.

The women around us are tucking in, scooping up rice with their right hand and quickly rolling it into a bite-sized ball. I have eaten like this with families in their gardens but Mansour always provides me with a spoon to avoid embarrassment. Today, I have no choice but to dig in, scooping rice from our shared platter as politely as I can. My fingers are all gluey and I have scattered the sticky grains of rice all over myself. I wipe the mess off my lap as discreetly as I can, conscious that grains are also gathering in the scarf around my neck. Harder to rectify and my attempts have just knocked a load down my cleavage.

Once the plates have been cleared and hands have been rinsed, it is time to dance. The Arabic music is turned up and the small girls rush to the dance floor. The young women soon join them, dancing like professionals, arms high, bangles jingling, and hips swirling. One lady smiles at me, beckoning me to dance, and the small girls quickly gather round tugging us to the floor.

"Oh no, no, no," says Lisa with a reluctant smile as she is pulled to her feet. I follow her, though I know that I cannot compete with these women, or even the children, who all dance like goddesses.

The three of us shake our stuff, failing to hit the beat of the music we opt for the familiar disco moves of the Macarena instead. It is great fun, everyone smiling and young girls twizzling all around us. We sit down for a pause and things suddenly become serious. Two exquisitely dressed girls face each other, a show down, both dancing with a ferocious intensity, showing off their rhythm, flexibility, and undeniable sexuality.

Similar scenes occur in the clubs on a Friday night back home, but there are always men present to see the display. Here it is the older women who are paying the closest attention, watching intently from the edge of the room, and whispering to one another. Which girl has the best body? Do they look like child-bearing hips? And does she know how to use them?

It is early evening by the time we get our first glimpse of the bride and groom. The marriage ceremony itself has gone on unseen, but now the young newlyweds are brought into the women's quarter to be admired by all. Before they arrive, the women around us cover up their brightly coloured dresses, replacing them with their black outer garments, which I now notice are decorated with subtle, delicate embroidery.

We all move outside, where the married couple are being guided through the crowd towards two throne-like seats that have been placed in the centre of the garden. The groom is wearing a smart galabeya, while the bride is dressed like a barbie doll, in an enormous white, glitzy wedding dress. Everyone calls and cheers as the couple sit down, but the young bride is weeping.

Her face is heavily made-up, pale skin, dark eyes, and red lips, with mascara now dripping down the sides of her face. The groom, a sweet looking boy, nineteen years old, squirms in his seat, attempting to engage with the stranger sitting next to him, trying in vain to make her smile or laugh. He gets no response.

After lots of clapping and cheering, the young husband and wife are then led into a small house at the end of the garden where they will be left alone to get to know each other. The girl's tear-filled eyes grow wide with panic and fear as she walks stiffly towards her unknown fate.

And with that, the wedding is over and we gather our belongings and head back to camp.

It has been a mixed day. Such wonderful feasting and dancing, but for what? As I lie in bed, I cannot help but worry, thinking of the two of them alone for the first time. I hope they learn to like each other.

Life is not fair.

# Chapter 10

I enjoyed being a guest at the wedding, but now it is my turn to act as host.

My mother is coming to visit.

I have been coming here for years now, talking endlessly to my family about the magic of the place, and I am nervous that it will not live up to my descriptions. What will she think of the dusty bedrooms, or of squatting down to sit on cushions laid on the hard stone floor? And what about Hamza and his creepy jokes, or climbing steep mountain paths in the hot midday sun? These questions all run through my head as I sit patiently waiting for her taxi to arrive.

My mum, Selena, feels tired and weary as her taxi pulls into Fox Camp. She had been met at the airport by a nice, smiling Bedouin man holding a scrap of paper with her name written on it, but the drive was long. She saw nothing along the way, the entire landscape hidden in the darkness,

So, she does not know what to expect. The camp is silent as she walks from the taxi. She looks around, just making out the shapes of the office and restaurant, and the pale neon glow of a F.O.X. sign that sits high above her on a rocky mountain slope. I jump up at the sound of the minibus pulling in and rush out from the tent to greet her.

We hug. A real hug, one that I do not want to end. When it does, I lead her to the tent, sitting her down by the fire. Hamza soon brings the tea, and we sit quietly, talking about her journey and the activities of my day. Hamza and I then show her to her room, where we hug again, saying our good-nights.

In the morning we meet for breakfast and I introduce my mum to all of my friends. She is polite, smiling and responding to all the small talk, but she does not have the energy to ask questions like she normally would. She feels flat. She has felt like this for months now. Perhaps it is the menopause, or because her children have left home for good. She does not know, she is just finding it hard to see the point.

My hope is that the mountains will restore her, lifting her back to her old self. I have plans to take her to the mountain gardens, but today is her first day so I have decided to keep things gentle. Instead of climbing up the rocky slopes, we stroll down the road to the Monastery of St Katherine. This is my third visit to the monastery, and although I have had enough of the tourist shops and the men trying to sell me bits of rock and crystal, I am still impressed by the first glimpse of the monastery. It lies hidden at the base of the valley, and the sight of the ancient walls and rows of olive trees emerging from between the mountains is undeniably beautiful.

Inside, the monastery contains history of biblical proportions. A rambling rose adorns the walls, an ancestor of the burning bush of Moses, and the chapel is heavily laden with icons and gold. For me, the most impressive treasures are hidden upstairs in the art gallery. We head up the steps and enter the cool, air-conditioned museum, where the man behind the desk leaps up and smiles broadly.

"Welcome, welcome!" he cries. "It is so very good to see you again."

"It is lovely to be back," I reply, smiling as my mum gets out the cash to pay for our entry.

"No, no," he says firmly as she hands him the notes. "For you it is free," he finishes, nodding at me.

We accept the offer gratefully, heading into the exhibition without paying the entrance fee.

My mum looks slightly bewildered. "Is that man a friend of yours?" she asks.

"No. I have no idea who he is, I am just famous here!" I reply. "Everybody knows me," I say with a laugh.

It is a joke, but it holds some truth. That man certainly recognised me, but I cannot place him. He may have once worked in the restaurant at the Plaza Hotel but I cannot be sure. Best thing to do is to smile and accept the kindness.

Our free entry gives us access to unmatchable Byzantine artworks, exquisite religious paintings, the stairway to heaven, and hand-written Bibles embossed with gold. Hidden in a corner there is a framed copy of a letter sealed with a handprint. It is a pledge for peace.

The handprint belongs to the Prophet Mohammed. It is his signature, his authentication of this letter, which contains his very own words of advice. Translated, he demands that all people who have respect for their God must protect the followers of Jesus, the Arabs, the foreigners, the known and the unknown.

This covenant has been held within the monastery since the very birth of Islam. It seems to have encouraged the Bedouin to work alongside the Christian monks, and in response the monks have built the staff a mosque within the monastery walls. Outside, people of the two faiths continue to live peacefully alongside one another, as if the sentiments of Prophet Mohammed have not been forgotten here in the town of St Katherine.

We fill our days with trips through the mountains, Mansour leading us up the zig-zagged path of Abu Gifa, down into the gardens of Wadi Tabuk and Wadi Zawateen. My mum slowly conquers the hot, rocky climbs and begins to loosen, absorbing the calmness of the valley.

Midweek, my surveys take us down into Wadi Itlah, through the wide sandy valley scattered with palm trees and up a rocky ridge towards the garden of Dr Khalid. Dr Khalid is a herbalist and knows everything there is to know about the mountains' medicinal plants. He is an old man, who speaks little English, but offers to show my mum around his impressive garden. He leads us through the immaculate rows of rocket, onion and fennel, past thick, glossy rosemary bushes, their scent wafting towards us as we pass. In the centre of the long garden, we pause beneath an aged carob tree, its trunk thick and twisted, and its canopy, heavy with carob seeds, wide enough to provide shade for at least twenty people. My mum gazes upwards at the spreading branches, lost for a moment, before noticing that we have moved on.

She catches us up as Dr Khalid leads us down to a block of toilets. He smiles proudly, gesturing towards the sinks, turning on the tap and running the clear water over his fingers. He is a smart man. As well as providing food for his family, this garden is regularly used as a campsite by groups of tourists. A few other garden owners have installed drop-toilets in their gardens, but nobody else has created such high-quality facilities with showers and sinks sourced from the local well water.

I spend the next hour surveying the plants and pollinators within the garden, while my mum sits quietly in the shade of the carob tree. She looks on, occasionally wandering over to inspect a bee buzzing in my net, or to gaze at a resting butterfly before it flits away. When I am done, we leave the garden and climb up the steep slope to Dr Khalid's stone hut, where he and Mansour have been catching up.

Dr Khalid and Mansour are brothers. It is hard to recognise this at first glance, as there are nearly two decades between them. Although the grey-bearded Dr Khalid is more ordered and purposeful than his younger, playful brother, they both share the same glint of wisdom in their eyes. He has managed to convince Mansour to build his own garden, a space to grow his own vegetables, fruits, and nuts. There is an apocalypse on the horizon, the old man is sure of it. When it happens, the lorries from Cairo will halt and the shelves in the shops will empty. He wants the people to be aware of this and feels secure knowing that Mansour now has the means to feed his wife and children. They need to become self-sufficient.

We interrupt their conversation, pausing at the door to remove our walking boots before sitting down on the hand-woven rugs. Dr Khalid welcomes us before going next door into his store cupboard where he collects a handful of dried rose petals. The two of them keep on chatting as Dr Khalid stirs the delicate petals into the bubbling tea.

Mansour concludes that his older brother may have a point. He lies back, rolls his home-grown tobacco and thinks about today's gardening tips, imagining how close he is to transforming the bare mountain rocks into a paradise of his own. While he dreams of the future, my mum is very much in the present. She sits awkwardly on the floor, but the flavour of the tea is calming and restorative.

I look at her and smile. Life feels simpler here. I hope that it is reminding her of how to live in the moment. Sometimes it is okay not to have a purpose; it is enough to just be.

## *Chapter 11*

Life is life, as Hamza always says, so while I am glad that my mum is enjoying the small things, I also think that she is in need of an adventure. It is time to take her away from the calmness of the mountains into the desert. This morning Qasim collects us from camp, Beth, my mum and me climbing in the back, Mansour shutting the heavy door before jumping into the front. We head off, stopping at the check point to show our passports before hitting the open road.

The plan is to return to Ain Hodra for my second round of surveys but on route Qasim takes an unfamiliar turning down a dirt track, leading us deep into the flat, rocky noth-ingness. After some time he pulls to a halt, stopping next to a lonely Bedouin tent, its roof made of strung together tarpaulins. He beckons us into the tent where we sit down on worn rugs, trapped beneath the hot black plastic roof. Qasim places a plastic bag full of vegetables, bread, and cheese in front of an older lady, whose black scarf is wrapped around her hair and face. She takes hold of the bag, gripping it tightly as she thanks him repeatedly, "Shukran, shukran, shukran."

Behind her, two girls emerge timidly, unwrapping a cloth parcel to reveal handmade bracelets and necklaces which they place in front of us, eager for a sale. A young boy clings to the lady's arm, wary of us strangers. When he steps forward, I see his face and gasp. The right-hand side is red and raw, pus oozing out of scabbed blisters.

I look at Beth and see that she is as shocked as me, both of us unsure what to say or do. My mum stays calm; she is a qualified doctor and has seen things like this before. Mansour begins talking with the mother, insisting that the boy needs antibiotic cream, which he promises to buy from the pharmacy in St Katherine.

I feel uncomfortable. I have visited dozens of families since working here, but I have never seen such poverty or isolation. This Garasha family are nomadic and do not have a garden or a permanent home. Instead they must pack up and move time after time, taking down the tents and gathering their few possessions before moving forward across the desert in search of new grazing land for their goats. The goats provide them with milk but I do not know how they get the money to buy other essentials.

Beth and I look through the items in front of us, picking up the occasional bracelet and politely commenting on its prettiness. I often get presented with handmade jewellery or embroidered purses and bags. Usually I just smile and say no thank you, but I cannot do that here. The girls and their mother are gazing at us intensely, as if praying that we will buy.

"Go on you two, try some on," says my mum encouragingly, helping us make a decision. We go for two matching necklaces, one pink and one blue, each with a little figure made of beads hanging from a simple piece of string. They are ridiculous, but I feel a sense of relief as we hand the cash over to this struggling family.

We say our goodbyes and get back on the road. The visit has shaken me, but as Qasim turns the music up and opens the windows, the cool breeze sweeps away the sense of guilt about my privilege and makes me feel free. The desert rushes past us and brings us once again to the cliff edge and the perilous path that leads towards Ain Hodra. Beth and I now have trust in Qasim's driving and we laugh as the Land Cruiser tips towards the drop. However, my mum, who had coped with the scabbed face of the boy, is now terrified. Her face is frozen with fear, her stomach knotted and the look in her eyes makes me start to regret bringing her here.

When we make it safely down to the palm-filled oasis she lets out a nervous laugh and feels the tension release. The oasis feels like a refuge, the perfect place to pause and regather. Of course, I need to work, setting off with my clipboard and net as my mum takes a moment in the shade. Beth follows me, helping me label tubes and keeping me company as I go, while Qasim and Mansour laugh and smoke with the camp owner. The sound of a Bulbul singing in a tree pulls my mum up and out into the oasis, where she weaves her way through the palms, running her fingers across their rough bark.

She is a gardener, so subconsciously maps the layout of the trees and plants as she passes. At home, our family garden is filled with colour and texture, roses winding over the pergolas, the orchard filled with daffodils and apple blossom, and the oak, horse chestnut and ash reaching tall into the sky. It used to be a cow field, bought thirty years ago along with the house, but now she has transformed it into something magnificent. This desert oasis could feel sparse and empty in comparison, but here, amidst the endless desert, this green haven is everything.

Once my surveys are finished, we drive out into the desert, settling in at the same campsite we visited before. Mansour collects the firewood, and Beth and I help Qasim lay out the mattresses. Then we all gather around the campfire, surrounded by nothing but the rolling dunes and the vast open sky. This is the same spot, but it feels different this time, strangely unfamiliar, as if in need of rediscovery.

"Who fancies a glass of Limoncello?" says my mum, holding up a pale yellow bottle of the Italian liqueur that she bought in duty free.

"What is this?" Mansour questions as he pours the drink into the small tea glasses. He sniffs it and takes a sip before he has been answered. He grins, immediately won over by the sweet lemony hit.

Around us, the night is beginning to take shape, the full moon rising slowly from the west as Mansour pours another round. He rarely drinks and is getting tipsier with every sip.

Once his glass is empty, Mansour leaps to his feet and raises it high in the air, before bursting into song.

"Limoncello, Limoncello. How I love the Limoncello," he sings, dancing around us as he goes. Qasim looks at him curiously, while the three of us smile and take in the moment. He continues to spin and laugh, as Qasim uncharacteristically leans forward and checks on the bubbling rice.

By the time the Limoncello is emptied and dinner has been eaten, we all lie together in the moonlight. The bright white moon is now high in the sky, and everything around us is submerged in its silvery blue glow. Beneath the blankets, Mansour takes Beth's hand, their fingers entwining with one another. Their eyes meet, sparkling, and instead of resting, Mansour pulls her to her feet.

There is madness in the air. Qasim and I follow the two of them towards the centre of the sandy valley, until Mansour stops and grabs hold of a thick, brown coat. He crouches down, hidden entirely by the fur lining, and undergoes a transformation.

He becomes a hyena.

It is a time when wolves might howl sorrowfully at the moon, but tonight Mansour has become something merrier. He runs on all fours, beast-like, chasing us across the sand in true hyena form. He makes us laugh and laugh and laugh.

Once the chase is over, the four of us take a seat on the soft white sand while my mum lies quietly alone by the fire. It is not a night for sleeping. The moon is getting brighter, and all around us everything is in sharp focus. We play like children, sat in a circle, using sticks to draw guessable images in the glimmering sand.

Our moonlit artworks will not last till morning, but the magic of this night will.

# *Chapter 12*

Two American tourists have just been kidnapped.

The two friends were heading back after a desert day trip when they were stopped, held at gun point and taken into the deepest desert by angry members of the Garasha tribe. The Garasha are demanding justice. They want the release of their fellow tribesmen, who have been unfairly arrested and detained by the Egyptian police. The plan is to swap the freedom of the two Americans for that of their family members, who do not deserve to be locked behind bars for crimes that they probably did not commit

While waiting for the Egyptian police to consider the situation, the kidnappers need to decide how to detain the two women. They drive further into the desert, with the women shaking in the back of the truck. They stop at a small hut along the way, where some sort of exchange takes place. The lead kidnapper slinks back into the driver's seat, concealing a package wrapped in a plastic bag by his side. He leads them onwards, through a deep rocky gorge into an expanse of scrubby desert. There is nowhere to run, no chance of escape, so the guns are packed away and the American women are treated in true tribal fashion.

The women are ushered out of the truck and sit fearfully in the darkness as the men prepare a fire. One of the men hunches down and flips out a shining knife blade. He slices open the plastic bag, revealing large hunks of raw goat meat. Since they are planning to keep these hostages for some time, they might as well enjoy themselves.

It is a night for a feast. The kettle is first on and everyone is served tea while the meat is slowly roasted on the fire. The men have been furious all day, incensed about the thought of their people in prison, but they soon begin to relax. The American women also begin to feel a slowing of their racing hearts, their panic fading and both feeling a rising interest in the situation they have found themselves in. They begin whispering to one another, building up their confidence before talking with the men. By the time the food is served, the whole group is laughing, exchanging stories from two different worlds. All appreciate the taste of the juicy meat that they are dining upon.

During the night there are lengthy discussions between the Egyptian police and the tribal Sheikhs, with the Gebeliya, the Muzeina and even the Garasha concerned about the impact that the event will have upon tourism. By morning, the kidnappers are talked round and, though still loyal to their cause, they release the Americans unharmed. The whispers and rumours spread quickly and within a couple of days everyone from the restaurants of Dahab, the beach huts of Nuwieba, to the mountains of St Katherine have heard about the experience of the two tourists. Though some of the gossip is fearful, the consensus is that they loved it. It gave them a real glimpse of true Bedouin culture and they are definitely coming back next year.

Here in Fox Camp these stories feel far away. I know that I was out there with my mum just a fortnight ago, but I cannot imagine a kidnapping happening to us. The Garasha men have issues with the Egyptian authorities, not with other tribes. The Americans were being driven by an Egyptian tour guide at the time of the attack and so were considered fair game. But we were being driven by Qasim. Qasim is a social-iser, well known across the region, with friends belonging to both tribes. Also, he is the brother of the Sheikh.

Anyway, the men have decided to move on from kid-napping. Instead, they have chosen to wind-up the police by cutting electricity cables out in the desert, disrupting ev-eryone's electricity supply. It is annoying and the police are really unhappy. They have stepped up their on-the-ground presence, with higher numbers of armed men stationed at the checkpoints both here and out in the desert. They have also banned tourists from travelling through the Garasha territory, a bit of a problem since this is where I have been surveying my other desert site, Wadi Fieran.

Qasim has assured me that he can negotiate his way through the checkpoints without any problems, and I trust him. So despite the risk, and the rules, I am heading out for the next round of surveys there, with Beth and Mansour join-ing us for the ride. We are waved straight through the first St Katherine checkpoint and we all share a buzz of excitement about spending another night beneath the stars. The music is turned up and Beth and I are chilling and laughing in the back when Qasim turns round and gives us an unexpected instruction.

"Get down. Lie beneath the blankets." he says firmly. I look at him, surprised and confused, and see that this is not a joke.

"Yalla. Quick, get down," he repeats. We do as we are told. We squash down between the seats, grabbing hold of the thick blankets and pulling them over us. I twig what is happening. Qasim is hiding us.

From beneath the blankets, I feel the car slow to a halt at the next checkpoint. Here the road splits, one road to the coast and the other to our destination, Wadi Fieran. We need to get through. There are five armed police officers at the checkpoint. One is on look-out, standing on the top of the building with his machine gun poised, while the others sit casually on plastic chairs. One gets to his feet as we approach, walking towards us with his machine-gun hung casually over his shoulder. Qasim winds down his window and starts explaining his reasons for entering the Garasha territory. The officer says little, but peers into the back of the vehicle before nodding and letting us through.

We were invisible. Nothing but a pile of blankets in the back. I begin to giggle. I know I should be scared, but it all seemed so easy. The barrier is raised and we drive on through, Qasim and Mansour laughing in the front, both looking straight ahead to avoid rousing suspicion.

Beth and I stay hidden for a mile or so, poking our faces out to get some air. When we are sure that we are out of sight, we throw the hot, suffocating blankets off, open the windows and enjoy the ride.

It is nightfall when things get more serious. The day was spent working in the gardens of Wadi Fieran, an isolated valley once considered magnificent by pilgrims and explorers. These days the gardens are dry, the palm trees all suffering, with many lying dead on the dusty floors. When I finished my surveys we came out to the desert to sleep in an open expanse that lacks the soft sand and moonlight of our last trip. We dine by the fire and part ways, Beth and Mansour disappearing into the darkness, leaving me and Qasim alone with one another.

Qasim and I have become an item, so to speak. Late at night we often wind our way back to my room, drunk, after hours singing and drumming in the tent. It is casual. We do not talk about our pasts or what we want with the future, but there is a different level of intimacy. When we are alone, he takes off his head scarf or cap, revealing the deep scar that runs across the left of his head. I do not dare ask him how he got it, but instead run my fingers delicately over the damaged skin and his shaven, soft hair.

Tonight, I move my head towards his and he pushes me away. He has a gun. He lifts up the corner of his pillow and shows me a revolver that has been hidden beneath him.

"I need it in case anything happens in the night," he says quietly.

I do not argue but shift straight back to my mattress. I feel a shiver of fear. There is no moon tonight, so I can see nothing around me, only darkness and stars. We are alone in Garasha territory, and anyone could be watching us. I understand now. The threat is real.

# *Chapter 13*

On a positive note, Sophie has had kittens. Earlier in the week, she had been sneaking into my bedroom and trying to nest in the suitcase under my bed. I hadn't let her, uncomfortable about the birthing process and associated mess taking place on the clothes that I store down there. Instead, the three balls of fluff have been discovered in an old shed at the back of camp, nestled between pieces of broken furniture, cracked wood, and rusty nails.

They are all healthy. One is tortoiseshell like their mother, one black and one black and white. The black one gets name after me, Zaytoona, Arabic for olive and the black and white one gets named Katkoot after Beth. When they are big enough to venture out into the camp, they are understandably nervous. Life is not easy for them here. Hamza taunts and teases them, yesterday placing them on a tray high on top of the refrigerator, the little things mewing desperately and unable to escape.

They need someone like Kevin to look after them. The camp is not the same without him. There used to be such a rainbow of cats surrounding him. He nurtured them all, including the one-eyed ginger tom cat that I adored, Simba. I remember when he discovered the bodies of his poisoned cats at the bottom of Wadi Shraig. It was painful.

After a couple of weeks, Lisa steps up, transferring her love of wolves on to the struggling kittens. Zaytoona is doing particularly poorly, getting thinner and weaker each day, while the other two are terrified of us all. Lisa explains that they need positive human interaction now, a bit of love and affection to ensure that they grow up to be confident around people. She is determined, starting with small strokes and tiny offerings of tuna. Before long she wins them over. The soft little kittens are now happily exploring the camp, winding between people's legs and content to be cuddled and stroked by us all.

The black and white kitten, Katkoot, is now Lisa's favourite, once feisty but now absolutely adored. The dear little black one has done less well, disappearing one afternoon last week. Hamza has just found the body, cold and alone in the corner of the old, cluttered shed.

## *Chapter 14*

Mohammed, a young and trendy Bedouin guy, pushes back his sunglasses, runs his hand through his hair and grins at the girl in his rear-view mirror. His mates are going to be so impressed when he arrives in the village with such a pretty, young American girl in tow. He picked her up in a bar in Dahab and offered her a lift to St Katherine. Now they are cruising up towards the mountains, which are glowing in the evening sun. It is night by the time he pulls into the camp. All is still and quiet, lit by the shimmering moon and the bright F.O.X. sign. The tent is empty, so Mohammed will have to wait until morning to show off his new lady friend.

It is very early in the morning when I am woken up by the sound of soft, delicate music outside my bedroom door. Intrigued, I step out into the pale blue morning light and see a slim girl crouched over the nearest flower bed, her mobile phone playing music at her feet. I watch silently as she gazes at the pink oleander flowers, her eyes glistening and her long, wavy hair catching in the gentle breeze. She notices me and stands up abruptly. She looks right at me, before her face melts into a smile.

"I am playing music to the flowers," she says brightly. "To help them grow," she explains.

"Ah, of course. Welcome to Fox Camp," I reply with a nod and a smile, before returning to bed.

When I wake up the second time, the girl and her music have gone. Instead, she is moving around camp, smiling brightly at everyone she meets and captivating them one by one. At midday, she is drawn to the small mountain behind the restaurant. She climbs the rocks quickly, with lightness, stopping only when she reaches the top. Up there she inhales deeply. Her arms stretch up into the clear sky, and her body follows as she rises onto her tip toes. She holds her breath. For a moment she wonders what it would feel like to jump and fly. Then her mind empties as she exhales.

Down here, Hamza and the other men have spotted the American girl. I stand up and join them, looking up at the poised figure whose curves are clearly outlined against the deep blue sky. She is now on one leg, her raised hands clasped together in prayer. She slips through the moves of the sun salutation, moving gracefully into the downward dog.

Her back bends, and our heads move. We are all transfixed. She does not notice us. Her mind is crystal clear, her breath filling her with energy and her body stretching itself to its limits.

As Lisa and Sean pass by, they too stop and stare. I have never seen yoga like this.

Word about her suppleness has spread quickly around town. The next day, there are unusual numbers of young men hanging around, including Mohammed and his friends. They are a day late. She has lost interest in yoga. Instead, she has been taken over by a religious spirituality and feels feverish about the thought of visiting the ancient monastery.

The girl paces around camp, running over the idea of the monastery visit and how it will bring her closer to God. Then she spots the tourist shop which now occupies the old cybercafé. It is filled with religious art works, images of the monastery, and of Jesus and his disciples taking the Last Supper. To my eye, the paintings look like crude reproductions, with thick brush strokes and cartoonish figures but to her they are a sign. The monastery can wait, today her calling is here in the camp.

Her creativity has been unleashed. She rummages unsupervised through the resident artist's possessions and then skips over to the terrace with her hands filled with brushes and paint tubes.

"I am going to run a group art class," she says gleefully, pulling the tables together and beckoning the men to join.

The men are won over immediately, sitting down in ordered rows and gazing up at her awaiting instructions. They are tasked with painting their names in Arabic script and they all get to work, keen to impress. The girl paces behind them, bending over closely to examine their paintings inadvertently giving them a peak down her tight-fitting top.

The class starts well, with the men focused on producing the neatest handwriting and the most elegant designs. They squabble over the tubes of paint, embellishing their works with gold and glitter. The teacher is not happy, she is striding back and forth with an increasing restlessness and then she snaps.

The girl sweeps their artworks to the ground. She grabs the largest brush and the blue paint, and then squirts it all over the tabletops. She uses erratic and forceful brushstrokes to create patterns across the surfaces, suddenly smiling with the sense of release.

The men step back in surprise. They are frozen. The tabletops are covered now in deep blue strokes. It takes several minutes before any one acts. When two of the tables are ruined and dripping with paint, the men act. They move the remaining tables out of the way, and together they gently prise the brush out of the girl's fist.

Something has shifted. People have become wary of the girl, who now talks with an intensity that is frightening. Her mind flips and wanders unpredictably and her iridescent eyes are piercing. She has talked to me about her psychology degree in Israel, about yoga, the power of poetry, and the Lord, but I have now started to avoid her, spending more time in my room so that we don't cross paths.

This evening, I walk straight past the tent, turning off my bedroom lights and hiding in the dark. It is too early to sleep, so I lie in bed reading with my head torch. I feel something. A presence. I look up and see her, staring at me through my small bedroom window, those eyes burning through me. She says nothing, and in a moment, she is gone.

She has left me a gift. I find it in the morning, a pair of earrings, two dream catchers, with bright turquoise feathers and pink beads hanging from the mosquito net on my bedroom door. It scares me. It feels like a curse, an omen of bad things to come.

I extract the earrings from the netting and look around for the gift-giver. I am on my own. I do not believe in black magic, so I need to get a grip. I close my fingers around the feathers and hang them from a pencil pot on my bedside table. I will accept the gift.

## *Chapter 15*

There is a full moon.

It hangs swollen and bright, casting a ghostly glow across the mountains. The American girl cannot sleep. The night is too bright. Thoughts are pumping through her. She needs to move. She feels trapped. She paces up and down the camp, past the rooms, past the tent, round and round the orchard.

The donkey brays. She looks up. The animals. They need to be freed. Her legs start running, pulling her towards the wadi. She opens the gates, releasing the horses, then the camel and the donkey. She calls, howls, wails, and together they gallop up and down the valley. She runs with them, hoofs and feet pounding the ground. Up and down the wadi. Every creature deserves to be free.

I snap awake at early dawn.

There is a wild scream, followed by a crash and the shattering of glass. I sit up in bed and shiver. The cry was barely human. It sounded like a psychotic soul locked in an asylum and desperate to break free. I run outside to see what is happening and find everybody staring at the girl. She is standing listlessly in front of the smashed shop window, a large rock and shards of glass scattered at her feet. From inside the shop, the eyes of the religious icons gaze down upon her, as if in judgement.

She now considers them blasphemous, fakes, faux religious art that is an affront to God. She was wrong to have been enraptured by them; they are nothing but money-making copies painted by an amateur's hand. She had no choice but to hurl the rock through the window; she had to put things right.

Things have escalated. No-one did anything when she had painted the tables blue. It was funny and it did not matter much. Now she has let people's animals run wild and caused real property damage. Something needs to be done. I want to call an ambulance. She is not well and needs to be taken into care before she harms herself or others. These emergency services are not available here, so I do not know what to do. I am too afraid to approach her, so just watch as she wanders groggily across the broken glass.

Cosmos, the old German carpenter, is the one who stands up and takes action. He is angry on a personal note, as she has interfered with his donkey and destroyed the shop that he built with his own hands. Later that morning, he comes into camp for the confrontation and we all gather in the restaurant area to watch the scene unfurl. The heavyset, white-bearded man trudges towards the crazy young girl, demanding an apology and a promise to cover the damage costs. Before Cosmos finishes his request, the girl has jumped up on her feet. I presume she is ready to run, but in one deft movement she whips down her trousers and bends down double.

"Fuck you, you fucking white man." she hollers, wiggling her buttocks aggressively in his direction.

The astonished audience blink at the sight of her bare bottom. My mouth gapes a little, and everyone around me sits in shocked silence. Her flexibility means she has bent so far that as well as her pale and round bum cheeks, I also have a clear view of her lady bits.

Many of the men start to laugh, enjoying the entertainment, and others applaud. Next to me, the innocent and unmarried gardener, Soliman, has a different response, his face draining with genuine shock and horror. Cosmos is understandably enraged. He raises his fist and shouts gruffly in her direction but she is off, pants up and running away from reality.

A few hours later the girl re-emerges, apparently oblivious of the chaos she has caused.

"I am going to give a poetry recital," she announces, climbing onto a prominent boulder to begin her readings.

She starts in a clear and confident voice, but very few stick around to listen. She perseveres nonetheless, standing high up on her perch for three whole hours projecting poetry to all who pass.

During the recital everyone scuttles around her nervously, whispering in hushed tones about what should be done. It is Farag who makes the decision. It is obvious. Young Mohammed had brought the girl here, so it is his responsibility to take her away.

Mohammed is the only one who wants to question the plan but, despite his usual cocky demeanour, he stays quiet and simply nods at Farag's request. He wastes no time and as soon as the poetry is over, he confidently approaches the girl and invites her on a trip to the monastery. She jumps at the chance, frenetic about the thought of connecting with God. She jumps in his car, taking nothing with her, her phone and all her belongings left in her room.

Mohammed locks the doors and drives straight past the monastery turn-off. It was a lie. Instead of showing her round the monastery he speeds straight towards the coast, where he can just dump her where he found her. Then she will be somebody else's problem. Sorted.

## Chapter 16

Things have slipped back to normal in the camp. I am no longer nervous, so have stopped spending my evenings hidden in my room and am out enjoying good company by the fire. The legacy of the crazy American girl remains though, with tales of moonlight and madness circling amongst us. Uncle Omar has been particularly affected by her visit and has taken a new interest in yoga. He had had the pleasure of a personal yoga session when the young girl had him lie down on the floor, pulled and stretched his limbs, and walked barefooted along his spine.

I call him Uncle Omar because he has the characteristics of an undeniably over friendly uncle. He is a rotund gentleman from North Sinai, who stays here in camp for months at a time working in one of the village shops. He is the one who gave Beth the nickname Katkoot, which translates as baby chicken, a sweet and fluffy little chick. For me, he calls out "Habasha, habasha, habasha", and chuckles deeply, holding on to his belly with both hands. I am a turkey, big, round, and feathery. I could take offence but he always manages to make me laugh.

His latest trick is to sneak up on me when I am sitting peacefully on the terrace. Without warning, he will take hold of my leg and lift it high in the air. He chants "Yoga, yoga, yoga." as he does so, finding great hilarity in it all.

Work is going well, though summer is approaching and the hours in the mountains feel hotter and longer. Beth is okay but is feeling increasingly uncomfortable with her guide Abdul. A few weeks ago he invited us all around for dinner. A kind act, perhaps, but it was not a fun experience. Beth and I drank too much wine beforehand to calm our nerves and then spent the whole evening sitting on the floor desperate for a wee. His children poked and prodded us with fierce eyes like their father, while the adults were serious. Nobody smiled. Eventually I asked to go to the toilet. It was a squat toilet. This would not normally be a problem, but in the places where I would usually place my feet there were two tall piles of breeze blocks. I tried to clamber up on to the blocks and squat from up high, but wobbled and nearly fell. In the end, the two of us just had to hold on to our full bladders for the duration of the horrible evening.

To distract Beth from worries about Abdul we are heading to Dahab for the weekend. This is a regular event, giving us a chance to lie by the sea in Yalla bar, drinking beers and smoking apple sheesha. The bar is filled with expats, tanned women with deep wrinkles over their faces and bikini-clad bodies. We do not fit in with their crowd, but the bar owner Remi is beginning to know us, and it is a great place to chill.

Our regular taxi driver, Hameed, arrives at camp within an hour of us calling, ready to take us to Dahab. He is a lovely, quiet man, who drives sensibly and carefully in his minivan, respecting all the checkpoints and the police. He is religious so will always stop if it is time for prayer. He calmly pulls over by the side of the road, lays his prayer rug on the rocky earth, washes his hands and feet with bottled water before praying towards the east. I try not to look, but the view of this old man kneeling down before the mountains is so moving. I have tried to sketch the scene, and keep meaning to paint it, but know I would struggle to capture its spiritual magic.

Hameed drops us at Bish Bishi, the cheap and cheerful hostel where we always stay. We usually get a warm and familiar welcome, but not today.

"Did you send her here?" the owner says angrily when he sees us.

"Who?" I reply, blinking at him and feeling confused.

"That mad American girl. They should have dealt with her in St Katherine, rather than just passing it on to us," he says angrily. "So selfish."

"Oh," I mumble. "Sorry. Nobody knew what to do."

We check-in silently. It turns out that she had taken a guest's laptop and smashed it over their head. I can understand why he is angry.

Like most of the staff in Dahab, the hostel owner is Egyptian, coming from the big city of Cairo. I get the feeling that most of these Egyptians do not trust or respect the local Bedouin, considering them unnerving, simple, tribal folk who do nothing but roam the desert. Last year, when Qasim had visited us out of the blue, the hostel owner had sounded suspicious when he told us that "some Bedouin" were waiting for us. He did not believe we could be friends.

Beth and I consider these attitudes stupid and feel bonded by our insider knowledge. We know so much about the Bedouin people, who are despised here. Often, we inadvertently entertain people with our stories. In the past we have been amused when the bar staff eavesdrop on our tales about Qasim and Mansour, or when tourists raise their eyebrows as we have talked tipsily about the challenge of getting romantic access beneath the traditional Galabeya dress. Yes, it is usually funny, but today I feel wronged by such blatant disrespect of the Gebeliya tribe, to which I feel a sense of kinship.

Our trip is quieter than usual, with Beth struggling to forget about Abdul and the discomfort she feels working with him. That evening, we sit at the sea front, the bright lights of the restaurants stretching around the coast, the stars faintly glimmering above us. Beth is not herself, holding her knees and gazing out to sea.

"Why don't you ring Mansour and ask him to find you another guide?" I say, knowing exactly what she is worrying about. Beth looks up at me, her eyes suddenly hopeful.

"Do you think he can do that?" Beth says.

"Yes, definitely worth a call!" I say as Beth gazes at her phone screen.

Beth dials Mansour's number and waits nervously as it rings. When he answers she blurts it all out. She is scared.

She does not trust Abdul. She cannot work with Abdul any longer. He makes her feel uncomfortable. She is sure he will do something to her. She just is not safe alone up there on the mountain with him. I thought Mansour would jump to her rescue, offering to sort it all out and find someone else to become Beth's guide, but he does not.

"Ah, Abdul is okay. He is quiet and strange, but hard-working. He knows the mountains very well, and he needs the job," Mansour replies casually.

Beth falls silent, and I take a sip of my wine. I feel bad that it is me working with Mansour; he should be with Beth.

Beth hangs up her phone and sighs. She could talk to Farag when we get back but the whole tribe are too connected. They will all ensure that Abdul keeps the job, because he needs the money to feed his children, everyone knows it. I give Beth a hug and we walk slowly back to Bish Bishi. It has not been our best Dahab trip.

# *Chapter 17*

There it is, a flash of blue.

The tiny butterfly flits between the thyme bushes before resting on a delicate white flower. It closes its wings, showing Beth its exquisite silvery underside, dotted with black and gold. They say that this butterfly is the smallest in the world, no bigger than your thumbnail. Despite its size, it has become an enormous part of Beth's life and as she squats in this high valley watching its movements she is completely absorbed.

Beth only has one month left of her studies and in this last phase she hopes to discover how goat grazing is affecting the health of the thyme plant. The Sinai Baton Blue depends on this plant, its larvae feeding on nothing else, and the Egyptian park rangers worry that the Bedouin grazing is a big problem. Beth is unsure and is determined to find out. For her, climate change seems like a bigger threat. As the temperatures get warmer, the plant and its butterfly can only survive at higher, cooler elevations. Together they have been shifting upwards, their range getting smaller and smaller, and if this continues, she worries that they will simply run out of space.

When the butterfly moves on, Beth continues measuring the size and health of the thyme plants. She does her best to concentrate, pushing away thoughts of Abdul, who is sitting alone at the site of their camp. She cannot quite explain why she has become so scared. Abdul has been her guide for three months now, leading her safely up the mountain and preparing reasonable meals. He has not done anything wrong exactly, never touching her or saying anything weird, but it's the stares. Now he is looking at her with an aggressive intensity, stripping her of her confidence, leaving her vulnerable and bare.

Beth works late into the evening, delaying her return to the camp. The sky darkens around her, making it increasingly difficult to make out the length of the thyme petals. Beth sighs and shivers. She cannot keep working and she is getting cold and hungry. There are no excuses not to return to the camp, so she slowly packs away her equipment, lifts her rucksack to her back and navigates her way up the rocky slope to the place where they sleep.

Abdul is crouched in front of the fire, a large black pot of rice simmering in front of him. He nods at Beth when she returns, saying nothing, no greeting or mention of the late hour. He serves up dinner and they eat silently, Beth forcing down spoonfuls of rice despite his close presence. As usual he clears up the plates, washing them in bottled water collected from the wells below. That is when it happens.

"Beth, I love you," Abdul whispers across the dying embers of the fire, his eyes fixed upon her. "I love you," he repeats firmly.

It is a statement, lacking flirtation or romance. Beth feels paralysed, wanting to run, but having nowhere to go.

"Beth, I love you. I love you. I love you," he says again and again, his voice getting louder and faster.

Beth is going to be attacked. Raped. She cannot think of another ending, or how to avoid it. Her mind is whirring, but she cannot think of anything to say other than the truth.

"I do not love you, Abdul," she says, avoiding his gaze and looking into the fire.

She waits. Her body is tense, ready for the assault but it never comes.

When she looks up Abdul has disappeared into the darkness. He is sobbing. He has buried himself beneath his blanket, his whole body shuddering with each cry. Despite the distance, Beth can hear the deep and anguished sobs. She stays sitting there until she is sure that he is not coming back and then moves away to her own mattress, even though she knows she has little chance of sleep.

She is terrified. She lies awake all night, constantly aware of his heavy breathing. Her body is frozen, avoiding any movement, in case it wakes him. At first light, she is willing to take that risk and begins quietly packing up her rucksack ready to escape. Around her the sky is still dark blue, but she can see enough now to find her way down the mountain.

Abdul hears the scrumpling of Beth's sleeping bag and snaps awake. He cannot let her leave here. She will tell everyone what has happened, what he has said. He is married. His wife cannot hear this. Beth cannot leave. Beth cannot destroy his life.

"You cannot talk of this. I am married. I have a wife and children," he shrieks jumping to his feet and lunging towards her.

Beth shrinks backwards.

"I won't, I won't, I won't say a word," she cries pleadingly, her voice cracking with fear.

Abdul is distracted. What has he done? What will they think of him? He collapses to the floor.

"My wife. My wife," he screams, lying face down now, bashing his fists and feet against the rock with each shout. He acts as a toddler having a tantrum. But one with the power and fury to cause Beth real damage.

Beth turns, and she runs.

I am woken up at 5 a.m. by the sound of my phone ringing. I look at the screen and see Beth's name. I answer immediately, with a rising sense of panic.

"I, I, I'm running down the mountain," Beth says, her voice hardly recognisable. This is worse than a scorpion sting. "Beth, it is okay, tell me where you are and what has happened," I say, trying to sound calm, even if my stomach is twisting.

"He... He tried to..." Her voice trails off. She cannot talk about it yet.

We keep talking, Beth telling me what has happened, her breathing heavy and thick with tears. She has the phone clenched to her face now and has called me as soon as she got signal. She continues to run down the mountain in the early morning gloom. Abdul has not followed her, but he is strong and fast and could catch her with ease if he changes his mind.

I throw off my blanket and rush through the empty camp towards the office. I keep the phone on me, listening to Beth breathing as she finds her way down the track, feeling reassured that she is safe and still alive. When I knock on the glass door, Hamza crawls out of bed slowly. As soon as he hears what is happening he finds a driver to go to the base of the mountain behind the monastery and bring Beth back to us.

Beth is safe. She has made it down the ancient rocky path alone in the semi-darkness and is met by the driver. She is guided gently into the car and driven back to camp. When she steps out of the car, I dive towards her and hug her tight. I wrap my arms around her shivering body and try not to cry. I cannot let go. This should not have happened to this incredible woman.

At the same time, Abdul is crouched on the mountain side, scanning the valley below him. He is hidden beneath a large, rocky boulder, his strong, muscular limbs tensed and ready to pounce. He is looking for Beth, but the entirety of Wadi Shraig appears empty and still. She had known he would pursue her. Even in the midst of her panic, she had opted for an unfamiliar route that they had never walked together, following the tourist trail which led her down to the monastery rather than to camp.

Abdul begins pacing, his patience wearing thin. Beth has outwitted him. Anger starts bubbling up inside him, his hands clenched into fists. His mind goes blank. He forgets about Beth and about his wife finding out what he said. Instead, all he feels is fury. He turns and throws himself against the boulder and screams with rage. The heavy rock tips, slowly at first, before tumbling down the cliff edge, creating an avalanche of smaller rocks as it goes.

The boulder lands with a thud. It has missed Abdul's original target, the intelligent and courageous Beth, who is now being spoilt in Fox Camp, getting the love and attention that she deserves.

# 2013

*Tea break*

# *Chapter 18*

It is just me this year. Beth has finished her PhD and new students are all put off by the post-revolution troubles.

Last year there had been a meeting after the Abdul incident and Beth had been allocated a new guide. Farag explained that the *Jinns*, evil spirits, were responsible for Abdul's actions. They had affected him once before when he had run naked through the valley. After pushing the boulder down in the hope of harming Beth he had gone home and attacked his sister. It was an unfortunate incident, but Abdul could not be blamed. It was the fault of the bad spirit.

Despite the new guide, Beth had finished her research but had chosen not to spend another night sleeping on the mountain.

Hamza and Uncle Omar are still here, along with other staff members who have become my friends. Apart from them, the camp is almost empty. There is a Russian nun, who dresses in black and commutes daily to the monastery, a mute Japanese lady who wears a floor-length purple Puffa jacket, and the occasional tourist. Since the revolution there have been real problems in North Sinai where there have been regular attacks on the Palestinian border. At home, the media has been talking endlessly of terrorism and chaos across Egypt, warning of Islamic extremism sweeping across the Middle East. Tourists have been put off.

I had also been anxious about coming back, but all my fears disappeared as soon as I got here. It felt like coming home. Those secret police do not come here anymore.

It had taken some work to convince the University to let me return. Endless forms needed filling in and risk assessments updating. I agreed to stop working in the low desert, in the oasis of Ain Hodra, and the gardens of Wadi Fieran, but am allowed to continue working up here in the mountains. Although I have been here a couple of days now, this is my first day back at work. I am continuing the same approach to my research, just tweaking the methods to improve the quality of the data that I collect. I have just finished breakfast and am waiting for Mansour to arrive. I smile at the sound of his dodgy, old moped pulling into camp.

"How is Beth?!" he cries excitedly as he sees me.

It is the first thing on his mind. After I answer, he remembers his manners, and greets me with a big hug. I have missed him.

Today we head into the village, an easy first day that does not require any climbing. I complete my surveys of the first garden and then sit down with Mansour, who has made me a strong, Arabic coffee, packed with sugar. Mansour knows that I love it. We sit peacefully for a good half hour, talking little but enjoying the sweetness of each sip and the warmth of the morning sun.

One thing Mansour does talk about is the floods. The rains came mid-winter, when I was with my family spending the evenings warm by the fire at our home. I had heard about it at the time, reading reports from charity workers explaining how the heavy rains had turned the wadis into raging rivers, causing widespread destruction and flooding homes.

Mansour's version is different. He is delighted. It had not rained properly for years. Now the dry wells have been replenished, the wadis are alive and, more importantly, his garden is thriving.

Over the coming weeks, I slip back into work easily. I remember the shapes and smells of the flowers and the sounds of the bees. I enjoy reconnecting with the gardens and their owners. So much is familiar, but the landscape has been transformed by the floods. When we head up Abu Gifa, I notice that the wide, zig-zagged path is crumbling. It used to provide essential access for camels, but the way has been blocked by fallen rocks and is in desperate need of repair. We reach the top and descend into the high mountain valleys which are vibrant and glowing. In places, the sandy soil has shifted and some garden walls have taken a blow, but the dried shrubs that had been nothing but brown twigs are now sprouting green leaves and coming back to life. All around me the wild herbs are bright yellows, purples, and blues, blooming with all of their might.

The gardens are also brighter, the trees greener and the herbs growing tall. On the mountainsides the women are herding greater numbers of goats and young kids. The rain has come at the right time. The crash in tourism has men out of work and families with no income, but the plentiful garden produce and goat's milk is helping them survive.

Down in the village there is one garden that has not benefited from the rains. When I carry out my survey there, I find that the plants have withered and the pollinators are scarce. When I finish, I sit down next to Mansour who is lying in the dappled shade of an almond tree.

"This garden is cursed," Mansour tells me.

He has been talking with the garden owner, who suspects that the spell has been cast by a neighbour who has always hated him.

"He found a whole egg, buried in the soil beneath this tree," Mansour explains, nodding up at the brown and lifeless canopy above us.

I am perplexed. I did not realise that people here believed in black magic, or that a chicken egg had the power to cause plants to wilt and die.

We finish talking and begin walking back through the village. Behind us, there are several cars queuing at the petrol station. I look back and see the worker in filthy clothes who is filling the drivers' cars one by one, inhaling the noxious fumes as he goes. I realise that the flash floods must have washed the station's grime and dirt down into the garden, polluting its soil with petrol. What a curse, no wonder the plants cannot grow.

I stay quiet on the walk back to camp, saying nothing of my thoughts about the petrol station. I think Mansour might believe it was the egg.

Life in camp is different now. I am not lonely, but I lack the security that I gained from having the other students around. And I have lost Beth, my partner in crime. Her namesake, Katkoot, is still here. He is the only kitten that survived. Lisa's efforts to charm him as a little one have worked, and he is now confident and friendly, jumping regularly on my lap and giving me the company I need.

I spend hours with Hamza, putting up with his poor jokes, and often sit quietly with Uncle Omar and gratefully accept his offered cigarettes. I also spend time admiring, and perhaps flirting, with Jamal, a young Bedouin man who works here. He speaks little English and works hard; he has twinkling eyes and knows how to make me smile. I remember catching my first glimpse of him at Qasim's family dinner party, where he passed quickly through the room greeting his family but not sitting to join us. Jamal is a brilliant drummer, outperforming Hamza. The rhythm of his playing entrances all in the tent. Oh, and he can dance. Beth and I had nicknamed him Peachy Bum, the only way to describe the wiggling of that bottom.

I have seen Qasim a few times, when he has chosen to rock up for a tent gathering. Things have fizzled between us. We talk and smile and sit together by the fire, but nothing more. It is not considered safe to travel down into the low desert to work because the Garasha are still causing problems, so I do not need him as a driver anymore. There are no longer regular desert trips, no more playing in the sand dunes or drinking limoncello beneath the stars. But it is okay. Life changes and things will be different this year.

# Chapter 19

Mansour's garden is beautiful. It is hidden at the far end of Wadi Itlah, squeezed in between the steep valley sides. There are bright purple flowers cascading down the hut wall, tidy beds containing all sorts of herbs and veg. The young trees are green and healthy, the nectarine branches heavy with plump fruits nearly ready to pick. Mansour's youngest son is crouched in front of the strawberry plants, giggling as he searches for the reddest and sweetest berries. His elder brother is standing quietly, fiddling with his head scarf, and watching me intently as I wander around the garden brushing the flowers with my fingertips.

I sit down and stretch out my legs in the warm afternoon sun. I have finished working but Mansour is busy. He is carefully inspecting his plastic irrigation pipes, checking that each plant is getting enough water. I smile at the little boy who is now running around me, shy, but keen to get my attention. The sky is deep blue. Behind the garden sits a woman wrapped in black, keeping her eyes on the dozen goats that move around her. She is Mansour's wife.

Mansour always waters his garden in the cooler parts of the day, early morning and evening. It is still too hot at the moment, but he plans to stay later and has arranged for his wife to walk me back in his place. Her name is Mansoura. Mansour shouts at her across the valley, and I feel nervous as she and the goats come in my direction. In the past, she has been rude and bristly towards me, knowing that her husband was cheating and suspecting it was me.

Mansoura and I set off together, leaving Mansour and the boys in the garden. She is larger and rounder than her husband, walking slowly and treading heavily on the uneven rocks. She begins chatting with me, asking me questions in Arabic about whether I am married or if I have a baby. Her voice is low and husky, but she seems interested and smiles as we talk. My return has not cheered her husband up, so she has decided to give me a chance. There must have been some other girl that had stolen him and made him so infuriatingly giddy with love.

After the small talk, we both fall silent and climb steadily up the mountain with the goats scattered around us. We wind around the mountain side, heading down into a smaller valley and past the gardens. Then there is one final push upwards towards their village, where a battered, white car waits to take me back to camp. The driver Hameed is scruffy and almost certainly stoned, but he drives slowly and safely and always treats me with respect.

Although I am becoming familiar with the mountain trails, I still often take a wrong path and get lost. Mansour is relaxing and often lets me walk parts on my own but knows that I feel safer with a guide. I have walked with a couple of guides other than Mansour, one of whom was a sleazy man who made me extremely uncomfortable. It was only one day of unwanted flirting but, from my response, Mansour made sure I never saw the man again.

This morning Mansour introduces me to his friend, Saad, who will be guiding me today. We set off up the zig-zagged path, Saad leading the way and seeming friendly and polite. He lives and works in the village, rarely walking in the mountains and soon gets out of puff. He stops often at convenient resting points, explaining to me how important it is to catch my breath and enjoy the view. He is right about the view, it is something, with the town of St Katherine sprawling out below us. We continue up at a sensible pace, before heading down into the flower filled valley where I begin my surveys.

At lunchtime we sit and rest in a garden overlooking the colours of Wadi Zawateen. Saad seems happy, taking in the mountain air and feeling a sense of freedom. After we have eaten, Saad begins to tell me a story.

"Have you tasted the apricots?" he asks, with excitement creeping into his voice. "The apricots are beautiful, so sweet. And there are so many up here in the mountains. After the apricots there is more—apples and pears," he continues, gazing up longingly at the small, unripe fruits that are hanging above us.

"Then later, there are the almonds, amazing. And then the figs. Oh, and I have forgotten the grapes, and the pomegranates, and the oranges!" he says dreamily, grinning like a small child talking about a sweet shop. "We are in paradise. This is the garden of Eden," he finishes with a contented sigh, lying back and taking it all in.

I get back to work, thinking about what Saad has said. He is right, this is paradise, with unmatchable diversity growing within these gardens. Ripe fruits and nuts from spring through to autumn, colours and textures, and fine flavours all through the year. This is how farming should be done. It is a long day, though, with the fantastic buzzing of bees and hoverflies within these gardens keeping me busy.

On the walk back I feel exhausted. I do not think I can manage the climb. Saad notices, and sweeps in, offering to carry my heavy rucksack and swap it for his, which is empty and light. I swap bags gratefully, feeling the air rush over my hot, sweaty back. It makes things easier and I perk up, climbing steadily and reflecting on what a kind and interesting man Saad is.

Mansour chats with his friend the following day, thanking him for looking after me and treating me well. He talks about his garden, how the trees are growing tall and how delicious and ripe the nectarines are. Saad's eyes widen at the mention of the fruit, and Mansour tells him that he is welcome to help himself next time he is in Wadi Itlah. This is a mistake.

Saad makes a special, purposeful trip to the valley, heading straight to Mansour's garden and the fruiting tree. He takes a bite of one, then two, then three of the juiciest nectarines and savours their sweet, sweet flavour. He starts grabbing handfuls, first filling his pockets, and then a cotton bag that he had brought just in case. Once his pockets and bag are full, he skips home, delighted by his bag of loveliness.

Mansour strolls down to his garden that evening to do the watering. He sees that the branches of his favourite tree are completely empty. He is not amused. He knows full well it was his fruit-loving friend and is fuming.

# *Chapter 20*

My head is thudding.

Bang. Bang. Bang.

It is not a hangover. It is a migraine.

My hand shakes as I take a sip of my morning coffee. Hamza is watching me. He watches everyone, gathering information about what they do, what they think and what they need. He has figured out that there is something wrong with me.

"Is it your head? I can give you a head massage?" he says.

I look at him. I would not usually allow this man to stroke my skin, but it might reduce the pain and right now it seems worth a shot.

"Okay, go on then," I mumble.

Hamza jumps up and places both hands on my head and begins. He rubs his dry, scaly fingers across my scalp, up and down, putting pressure on my throbbing temples. It works. Men here know how to massage. I do not know where they are taught or how they pick up the skills, but massages are always offered, an ideal way to touch and get intimate with a woman.

Hamza's hands begin shifting down my neck, squeezing my shoulders. It feels good, relieving the tension in my muscles, but I know exactly what he is up to and where his fingers are likely to be headed.

"Hallas, enough," I say, bashing his hands away. "Shakrun, it did help," I add, thanking him, because it felt good and temporarily distracted me from the pain.

My migraines start with an aura. A blob of out-of-focus vision, or a glimmering zig-zag that floats gradually from side to side. The aura lasts about half an hour, taking all my attention and making me blind. Then there are the headaches, usually only an hour or so of unbearable, stabbing pain, which I know will not last too long. The worst bit comes afterwards, when I am wiped out, tired, flat, and unable to think or speak in the way I want to. This can last for days.

"I have a new idea," says Hamza later that day, approaching me and uncapping his hands to reveal a packet containing hashish.

It is compressed cannabis resin, stronger than the usual joints, but right now I am willing to take a risk. The two of us head to the office for some privacy, where Hamza balances the hashish in the centre of a small cup. He lights it, placing another cup on top, the smoke building up beneath the glass. I have seen this happening before, occasionally joining in in the tent, so I know what to do.

Hamza moves the glass cups towards me, opening them in front of my lips. I inhale deeply and the white smoke spirals into my lungs. My mind empties.

I feel total release. The heaviness that was crushing my mind has lifted. Dreamlike. A sense of peace.

I have had mixed experiences with cannabis in the past. When I smoked alone with Iqbal I was safe and giggly, but other times I have felt paranoia. My apple sheesha pipe was once spiked with hashish, making me scramble to my room, lock my door, and rock slowly backwards and forth late into the night. Today, the strong hashish is exactly what I needed. It is far more effective than my traditional remedies of Paracetamol or Ibuprofen, and my oppressive fatigue has been replaced by a lovely fluffiness.

The hashish fades and the day passes by in a slow whirl. When I feel like this I can never work properly. Sometimes I do simple and repetitive tasks like data entry that require no thinking, but today I do nothing. I just laze in the tent, felling weak and dazed as I wait for my mind to resharpen.

My energy does come back. The following day, I feel well enough to survey gardens in the nearby village and after that I am ready to climb. Since the political instability and terror threats have stopped me working in the low desert I have now extended my surveys into the higher mountains, into a new valley named Wadi Tinya. The walk takes us through the wadis of Tabuk and Zawateen and then past the impressive peak of Gebel Abass Basha, which is crowned by the ruins of an unfinished palace. Mansour and I stroll casually past this piece of history, where the large rocks that were moved at the request of an Ottoman Emperor now merge into the landscape.

Wadi Tinya is a long and wide valley filled with big orchard gardens that many families move to during the hot summer months. At the far end, there is a newly built dam designed to capture the rainwater from the flash floods. It is impressive, filled with deep, dark water that stretches between the rocks. A lake that looks out of place in the arid surroundings.

Mansour and I are staying up here for two nights so that I can complete my surveys in one go. We are being hosted by a family who are based here, living on food that was brought in by camel, and on the fresh produce from their garden. Once I have finished my day's surveys, we sit down and are served sweet mint tea by the kind lady of this garden. Her teenage daughter comes out of the hut wearing bright colours. Her hair is covered by a scarf but her face is open and smiling. I get out a bottle of suntan lotion and hand it to the girl who thanks me excitedly, gripping the gift tightly before running off into their hut to try it out.

The following day I sit for lunch with the lady and her daughter, while Mansour is off collecting dried plants to feed the camel. As her mum chops our salad, the girl stares at her smart phone, messaging non-stop. There is a boy she likes. The new sun cream is sure to boost her chances, making her skin soft and light. Once we have eaten, the girl jumps up and asks her mum if she can go out for a walk. She wraps her pretty purple scarf around her hair, a couple of dark strands peeking out at the front, and smiles at me, waving as she heads out. She is not allowed to speak with the boy, but if she passes his family's garden at the end of the valley there is a good chance that he will catch a glimpse of her, and hopefully he may like what he sees.

Her mother tidies away the plates, puts the kettle on the fire and then sits down next to me and begins to chat. The first time I met her I had thought she was older. The men had been there, so most of her face had been covered by her black scarf. Now it is just the two of us, I can see that she is young, perhaps only five years older than me. I have practiced my Arabic, taking classes back at home, so now we are able to understand one another. She talks fondly about her daughter, telling me that a man had wanted to marry her and had given her the phone as a gift.

"But she is so young," I say, using my basic Arabic, shocked that this girl will be expected to marry at her age.

The lady laughs. "She will not marry him, she just gets a great present," she chuckles.

I nod slowly, trying to comprehend this. The girl is able to accept expensive gifts from admirers, but not spend time with the boy she fancies. Their lives are so different to mine.

"Do you have your own phone?" I ask her and she shakes her head.

"I have no phone. I cannot use them," she replies. "I cannot read," she finishes.

I try to stay positive.

"Mafish Mushkala. No problem. You have an amazing daughter, a beautiful garden and live here, in these beautiful mountains," I say, gesturing towards the unmatchable views that surround us.

She looks me in the eyes and sets me straight.

"Fi mushkala. I cannot read," she says calmly, but firmly.

I am an idiot. What was I doing pretending that her life is okay? This lovely, kind, and clearly intelligent woman cannot read. She has not been given the education she deserves.

This is a problem.

## Chapter 21

Christine is locked in a bare concrete room, in the house of a man that she does not know. She is an artist who flew from New Zealand to Cairo in search of inspiration. At the airport, the man had offered a free place to stay, and she had gone along with it, looking for an adventure. It had not worked out so well and now her priority is to escape. She gets her chance when he visits her with food and forgets to lock the door. She slips out into the night. Luckily enough she still has her debit card and passport which she had kept hidden from him and she is free to travel wherever she likes.

The logical place to go is St Katherine. It is the land of Moses and spirituality, and she is sure she will be safer there. To make sure similar problems do not arise again, Christine decides to alter the way she dresses. She buys a long, floor length garment and wraps her black scarf around her head. She finishes her look with dark sunglasses and wears her new bum-bag around her waist to keep her possessions close and accessible. The coach trip to St Katherine is direct and she finds a tourist camp at the far side of town. She settles in quickly, glad to have a base from which to explore.

The staff are friendly and welcoming, but problems soon arise from their cooking. Christine is a reasonable woman, who enjoys a fried egg with her breakfast. She has asked politely each morning, but the men do not seem to understand the word fried. After an entire week of omelettes and scrambled eggs, Christine has had enough. She needs to make a stand.

She strides into the kitchen and explains firmly to the chef that she needs a fried egg. The man looks at her blankly. Christine has no other option; she lifts her loose top and exposes her white breasts.

"Please can I have a fried egg," she says slowly and loudly.

"A fried egg looks like this." she follows, pointing directly at her nipple, which clearly represents the egg yolk.

It works and she gets her dream breakfast. However, things become awkward after that. The staff get overly friendly and are desperate for a repeat of the egg incident. Christine cannot tolerate it, so packs up her bag, covers her hair with her head scarf and walks out in search of somewhere new.

The two of us pass unknowingly in the street, I am headed to the mountain and she to Fox Camp. When I get back, we are introduced by Hamza and start to get to know each other. She talks casually about her escape in Cairo and before long it becomes clear that there is one thing on her mind. Sex. She talks openly to everyone about related topics, discussing the attractiveness of various men, the usefulness of condoms and the fun of a clitoris.

Her first plan is to seduce Farag. This is an unusual choice, with most women, me included, considering the younger men who hang out in the tent to be more attractive. Farag is a married man. He goes home every night and spends his time in camp focused on his work. He rarely sits in the tent other than on the occasions when he is hosting important discussions with Sheikhs, army officers or police. Christine watches him from the terrace, telling Hamza and me that this man is a catch.

Over the next few days, I watch as Christine makes her move. Farag spends most of his time in camp pacing around and talking loudly on his phone. I am sitting at the bamboo table, with Katkoot running his soft black and white face against my fingers. In front of me, Farag is walking back and forth. Still dressed in a winter jacket, he is a heavyset man with thick, curly hair falling around his shoulders. Christine leaps in front of him, still wearing her modest gear she smiles and flirts with all of her might. He is not distracted. He simply nods and continues on his way.

She is persistent but becomes frustrated that Farag cannot be swayed. Her next target is Qasim.

Qasim is getting married. I only found out when Beth visited me a few weeks ago. He had said nothing to me, but told her the day he saw her, wanting her to pass it gently on to me. I don't mind, no, really, I am happy for him. We had fun last year but it was never serious, and he is past the age where people expect him to marry. I have been invited to his wedding. I do wish him the best.

Anyway, I have a new distraction that Christine is un-aware of. Jamal, with the sexy bum, has started paying me a bit more attention. I have been pulled into a game that I should have played as a child, where he catches my eye and grins in my direction, or sits beside me holding my hand secretly beneath the table. I cannot keep my eyes off him, gazing at him as he serves tea, clears the plates, sweeps the floor, plays the drum, dances like a dream or pulls into camp on his brand-new motorbike. It is silly, but I am smitten.

There is no privacy in camp. Jamal and I are never alone, passing briefly in the restaurant or sitting collectively with Hamza, Soliman and other guests by the fire. This evening, Jamal calls my name, drawing me out of the tent into the darkness. He speaks very little English, but manages to ask me to join him and his friends on a late-night walk. I say yes and follow the three men up the rocky path that leads to Jamal's family garden in Wadi Shraig.

This is my favourite garden. It is just a short ten-minute climb from Fox Camp, but once there you are transported to a different world. At the start of the scramble you can see the main road, see the street lights and hear the cars passing by. By the time you reach the garden, the outside world is hidden. All you can see is mountains and sky.

Every time I come here, I feel contentment. The very first time, I was invited in to eat barbequed chicken by a kind family I did not know. Then I remember coming here with Iqbal, when the two of us lay beneath the mulberry tree, with all those dripping, red berries heavy above us. It always changes. Tonight, Jamal has laid out the rugs and we all sit beneath the stars. His friend, also called Jamal, is rolling a joint. It gets passed round, each of us inhaling deeply, one puff after another.

I lie back. The stars are looking brighter than I have ever seen them. They dip in and out, flickering, twinkling, the world shifting, everything in flux.

Time passes.

The moon begins to rise. I watch as the white glow emerges from behind the rocky mountains, and the disc rolls slowly through the sky. White, so bright. It alters the colours of everything around us, wrapping us in a dreamy haze.

"Gamar gameel," I say to the men around me. The moon is beautiful.

I start giggling. This world is so magnificent.

There are murmurs of agreement and my ongoing laughter shakes Jamal awake. He decides that we all need tea, so jumps up and goes to the well to pull out water. He leans over and lowers the bucket into the water and hears a light plop. It is not the bucket but his mobile phone, which has slipped out of his pocket.

Jamal needs his phone; it is his life. He will have to climb down and get it. He pulls off his galabeya, which is too long and will get in the way. He stands there for a moment, his toned chest glimmering in the moon light. Then he begins climbing down, using his strong arms and legs to hold himself between the walls. He descends slowly, getting deeper and deeper, and closer to the water. Feeling as if he is being swallowed up by the stone walls which now tower above him.

Up above on dry ground we hear a splash. Jamal's friends run to the well edge. He has slipped and fallen into the water, but has managed to rescue his phone as he did so. Jamal is stoned. Instead of panicking, he grabs the rope tied onto the bucket using it to pull him from the dangerously deep water, and then clambers up the rocks. When he makes it to the top, he climbs out, stands on the well wall and shakes his wet, curly hair, laughing with relief. He could have died.

Jamal's friend grabs him by the shoulder and guides him back to the rug, wrapping his shivering body with a blanket. His other friend takes over the tea making duties. Jamal's phone is soaking, probably broken, but Jamal is okay, so we laugh, drink tea, talk and smoke until the night begins to fade.

I am tripping, sliding, and stumbling on the walk back down, feeling giddy and happy. It is Jamal's friend, not Jamal himself, who puts out his hand, wrapping mine in his and guiding me carefully down the rocky path. Jamal walks at a faster pace, disappearing off ahead of us. When we reach camp, the sky is orange and all is quiet. Jamal and his other friend are sat waiting for us. They get to their feet when they see us. We whisper our goodbyes, waving and dispersing, Jamal and I going in opposite directions. I stand by my bedroom door for a moment, looking up at the light of the morning sky, and then turn, stepping inside and burying myself in the dimness of my room to sleep.

# Chapter 22

Apparently, the UK media is making a fuss about Egypt, reporting that people are getting angry about the unwanted political change. Since the revolution everyone feels freed and able to talk openly about what is going on. Now they can disagree with the President's decisions and consider who they would prefer to be in charge. Morsi won the election, but he is pushing the ideology of the Muslim Brotherhood and people are angry about the loss of liberalism. They have scheduled a second revolution, another protest planned in Tahir Square to demand further change.

When I spoke to my parents this week, my mum sounded nervous about what is going on. I do not share her nervousness. Indeed, I have been whipped up by people's attitudes and understand their need to protest. People demand freedom, wanting to manage their jobs and land without interference. But I am scared of the violence and the scenes of chaos that I have witnessed on the Egyptian news, like the images of a mad man on a tall monument who had grabbed a boy by his arm and flung him to the floor. The little boy was not upholding the man's religious standards and so the man believed he deserved to die. This is not right. Things need to change.

None of the violence has reached us in the mountains. Today is revolution day but I am working as normal. After surveying a few gardens, I sit for tea with Mansour and a garden owner, relaxing and enjoying the shade of an almond tree.

"The protest started six minutes ago," says the garden owner, looking at his watch.

Mansour nods supportively and inhales on his roll-up, and I take another sip of the sweet tea. We have been talking about it non-stop for days but have completely missed the start time. We are sheltered by mountain life, protected from the riots that are beginning in the streets of Cairo. There are men and women being crushed in the crowds of Tahir Square, but my day goes on as normal.

Later that afternoon, I sit on the terrace, typing in my data and inhaling on a cigarette. I never used to smoke. I thought it was a terrible habit that did nothing but kill. Here I have so much time to fill, so little to do, and it suddenly feels worth it. A simple pleasure. As I stub out the shameful cigarette, I hear something tap on the table beside me. I look up and see Kareem who is gifting me a crystal that he has found in his garden.

Kareem has been back home in St Katherine for a month or so. He has come from Slovenia, where he has been living with his wife and young daughter for the past five years. He is the brother of Jamal and is one of very few Bedouin who have married a European and moved abroad. Things were very different out there. He had needed a break and had an unquenchable yearning to be back here in the mountains.

Now he is back, he has started paying me attention, presumably unaware of my flirtations with his brother. Most afternoons he comes here, placing chocolate, biscuits, crystals or flowers in front of me. I hardly know this man and these casual offerings are doing little to warm my heart. He often sits near me, joking and telling stories that he has shared with dozens of female tourists in the past. He is failing to seduce me, but his company is becoming a familiar ritual and I do enjoy munching on the biscuits.

Christine pops up, attracted by the presence of a new male. Kareem looks at her with interest and suggests that we all climb Wadi Shraig, a good way to fill the early evening and to get to know each other. He is right and there is nothing else to do except data entry, so we all set off together. We do not head to the garden, but instead settle beneath a big, impressive boulder on the right of the valley. As Kareem begins collecting twigs to light a fire for tea, Christine pushes the conversation into unfamiliar territory.

"What do you think about female genital mutilation, Kareem?" she asks.

He stops, and looks up at her, his eyes widening.

"Kareem?" she repeats.

"When they cut off lady's clitorises to ruin their sexual pleasure," she continues, clarifying things for him.

I am more shocked than Kareem, who starts to laugh.

"It happens all over Egypt, but you are right it makes things harder in bed," he responds, giving Christine the eye.

The conversation continues explicitly, discussing how here they only chop off the very tip of the clitoris, whereas in other parts of Egypt things are worse, with many women suffering from scarring, horrible pain during intercourse and difficulties during childbirth.

Christine is excellent at discovering things. I have lived here for years and had no idea that this went on. Her confidence in talking about the mutilation of teenage girls has taught me so much. I now know how it is done, who does it, and what it does to the victims. Disturbingly, it is Kareem's mother, the village midwife, who does the cutting. It is appalling. There are women here who have not been educated, who cannot read, and are not allowed to leave their house. On top of this, they have been forced to have their clitoris cut, sentencing them to a lifetime of discomfort and pain, with no opportunity of sexual fun and much needed relief.

Christine is also extremely confident at pursuing sex. She has no interest in Kareem or Hamza and has moved on from Farag who would not respond to her advances. Instead, she has been looking around outside camp. She had great success taking the virginity of a young lad on the ground, outside the monastery where he works. Then she had arranged a desert trip with an older, hunkier man, but he had been too forceful and wanted more than she was prepared to give. There was also a guy in Dahab. She had met him online and had asked me to guard her laptop as she ventured up into his flat. He was a great shag but she had been sure he would have stolen her laptop.

Her next project is to seduce Qasim. Yes, he is about to get married but this just means she needs to be quick. She knows my history with Qasim and I feel a bit possessive when she tells me of the plan. I raise the issue of his future wife's feelings but Christine is undeterred and secures an invite to Qasim's flat. On the night before the wedding, she sits smugly on his plush floor cushions but she gets nothing from Qasim other than tea.

Christine and I are both invited to the wedding, so the following day we walk into the village together. I am wearing a dress with a scarf around my neck, while Christine has her hair covered and looks far more respectable. Once again, women and men are separated and we are guided into a tent filled with sitting women and energetic young girls. The music starts and the small children dance around us, but it is early and I am not ready to join them. It feels different to the last wedding, perhaps because my friends are not with me. I am feeling uncomfortable about the thought of seeing Qasim with his bride and Christine is twitching. In an hour, she has had enough and stands up ready to go home.

"It is nothing but a children's party." she says in a huff.

I suspect things will change with the food and the after-party, but she has a point. Without Christine I will have no-one to talk to so I get up and join her, smiling awkwardly at the women, and sneaking my way out with her.

It is a relief to be out of there. I want Qasim to be happy, but I feel a knot in my stomach at the thought of him marrying another woman. He had a choice of two women, a lady his age who has lost her husband or a younger, prettier lady. Mansour tried to convince him to pick the widow, who is kind, intelligent and has a great sense of humour, but Qasim has gone for the pretty one. Only time can tell whether they are a good match.

When we get back to camp, Hamza can see that the wedding is bothering me and has the perfect distraction.

"Yalla Habibi, yalla," he whispers, beckoning me into the restaurant and closing the doors gently behind us.

He has made an ingenious creation with help from a Russian tourist, which the two of them were planning to try out while we were at the wedding. It is an enormous bong, made from a bucket of water and a plastic bottle. Given the circumstances I am invited to join in. The hashish is lit, and the three of us inhale the enormous clouds of smoke. Although I have smoked joints before, today there is an entire bucket filled with the pungent aroma of marijuana. I have never done anything like this before in my life.

We take a break and go out to the terrace, where Christine has been sitting on her own. She is glad to see us but soon becomes irritated at our shared hilarity. Around her, the three of us laugh and laugh and laugh. She cannot work out what is so funny.

Suddenly, I hear a gun shot.

Then another, bang, bang bang-ba-bang, bang.

I freeze, fighting a wave of paranoia, before realising that it is part of the wedding. The noise continues. Above the tents the heavens are filled with the flare of gunshots, family and friends shooting high to celebrate the marriage of Qasim and his beautiful wife.

If I had stayed, those bullets could have rained down upon me from the sky. Christine was right to make us leave early. Thank goodness I am here, stoned, and safe in Fox Camp.

# Chapter 23

I wake to the sound of scrabbling at my window. I sit up and see that it is Katkoot, scratching determinedly on the netting. I let him in and he jumps straight onto my bed. He rubs his face against mine and then stretches out by my side. I love this cat. I snuggle up beside him and sleep contentedly. It is great to have company.

Life in camp has got even lonelier. Things with Christine are frosty, and Jamal will not say a single word to me. After the wedding, I had been chatting to Christine about my own love interests, opening up about my crush on Jamal, telling her how we had secretly held hands and kissed in the camp's olive grove. I did not mean to perk her interest, but she immediately took notice of him, finally spotting that beautiful bottom and his ability to sway and dance. She seduced him without a problem and told me all about it, making me feel kicked and rejected,

I was hurt.

When he asked me what was wrong, I had called him stupid. When he looked blank, I was pushed to add, "because you fucked Christine!" I did not get an apology. He was furious and stormed out of the office. He has not spoken to me since.

Weeks have passed, but Jamal still avoids me. He swerves or changes directions when he sees me or treats me like I am invisible. When he cooks shared meals that I used to be invited to join, he keeps placing the dish at the far end of the table, eating grumpily with the men and not looking in my direction. It is upsetting, but I do not need Jamal. In the evenings, I still have the company of Hamza and Uncle Omar, and at night, Katkoot has made a habit of sleeping in my room.

Jamal has moved straight on to another love interest, a local girl from the village who he talks to endlessly on the phone. He now avoids the tent, instead locking himself in his room for hours, telling her how beautiful she is and showering her with praise. His wife does not get any of this attention, and feels abandoned as she spends days and nights alone with their child. She did not hear anything about his antics with me and Christine, but rumours about his relationship with this local lady are being whispered all around her. Many are insisting that her husband marries this girl, bringing her into their house as a second wife. She shivers every time she hears this gossip. It would be unbearable.

Jamal is sleeping more than he used to. It is due to the opium, the poppy resin that he has started taking regularly to dampen his confusion and pain. He does not know what to do about the second marriage and the opium frees him temporarily from his worries. To everyone else, it has made him flat, an empty shell lacking sparkle. He now reminds me of the opium addicts that hang out in camp such as Jumar. Jumar is a silent man, with heavy eyes and a droopy moustache, who drives all the way from the desert to lie in the Fox Camp tent, curled beneath a blanket for hours upon hours.

The poppies are grown in gardens across the valleys, beautiful flowers with big petals of pink or purple that are buzzing with bees. Once the petals have fallen, it is easy to extract opium, putting vertical slices in the green, round ovary and making sure the plant has enough water. With time, the white liquid oozes out and turns a golden, sticky brown in the hot sun. It is now ready for harvesting. People grow them in low numbers, rarely thinking about them, just feeling glad to have them for medical reasons and use in family emergencies.

Since tourism has dried up, the number of poppies has increased. Some people have started growing them on the rocks outside their gardens, creating strips of intense pink throughout the wadis. They are also being grown in huge numbers lower down, with large fields of bright flowers hidden within the miles of dry desert. There is enough water this year following the winter rains, but in the long term this type of farming will drain the wells and put real limits on the productivity of gardens in Wadi Fieran.

As well as draining water supplies, opium-growing is illegal. Nobody ever minded a few pretty flowers growing in the mountain gardens, but the police have started paying strong attention to the opium fields. The thing is, people have lost their source of income, they have no money, and they have no choice other than to take this risk. It is hard work down in the desert farms, requiring hours of back-breaking work harvesting hundreds of flowers in the heat, but it gets them money. The opium is sold on to drug dealers who then sell it in Cairo, making a fortune, paying the farmers only a small fraction of their profits.

Mansour once dreamt that he grew opium, that he was rich, rolling in cash, and his garden was filled with rows of the bright pink flowers. He dreamt that he was cooking a feast, with big metal pots simmering on the fire. But when he opened the lids he saw that the pots were filled with bodies: his family and friends were being boiled alive. It taught him never to sell opium. Yes, it can make you money, but it is highly addictive and you never know who will get hooked, or whose life you will destroy.

Let us hope that Jamal soon learns his lesson.

# *Chapter 24*

Mansour and I are on our last trip to Wadi Tinya. It was a hot climb, but up here the cool mountain breeze gives a little break from the summer sun. The gardens and houses are full of families who have moved up here for the school break, their chatter and laughter ringing through the valley. Despite all the people, the dam is now empty, with nothing but pools of green water along the base. The rest of the dam water has sunk into the cracks and crevices beneath us, filling the garden wells and allowing life to flourish.

I work slowly, moving between the gardens and the rocky surroundings. Mansour floats around, hidden from me, until he knows that I am in need of a rejuvenating cup of tea. He is also there when I need to move further down the wadi. We walk together, passing young girls in brightly coloured dresses looking after their goats.

Mansour leads me to an empty hut, where he makes lunch and then suggests a post-prandial nap. I never used to sleep during the day. In the desert, Mansour and Qasim always lay beneath the shade after lunch, pulling their scarves over their faces to keep off the flies. They both slept content-edly, while Beth and I whispered energetically, waiting for things to restart. This year Mansour has converted me. Most days I nap after lunch, finding the shadow of the greenest tree, placing my bag behind my head, and slipping straight off to sleep.

It is hot. Despite the fresh mountain air, it is still essential to identify the coolest sleeping spot. Mansour settles on the inside of the stone hut, which is high on the valley edge and filled with dark shadow. I copy him, lying on the opposite side of the small room. The air is sticky, but Mansour drifts straight off. His breathing is deep and heavy. He often talks in his sleep, feeling anxious and trapped, unable to escape from his horrible dreams. But today he is calm. His familiar breathing soon settles me. In and out, in and out,

Then the earth moves.

I open my eyes. The entire valley shifted beneath me,

"Mansour, did you feel the earth move?" I ask him quickly.

"Yes, yes, yes. It is no problem," he mumbles, slipping straight back to sleep.

I lie there, reflecting on what has happened. The floor beneath me had dropped, the rocks of the mountain jumped, just for a moment. It was an earthquake. Perhaps I should panic or scream, but there is nothing I can do about it, no way to escape. The rocks have stilled, so I close my eyes and like Mansour, I head straight back to sleep.

After napping and surveying pollinators, we make our way back to the garden that we stayed in previously. The lady's whole family has joined her now, her younger daughter and her husband. I felt so out of place the first time we stayed here, but now I am blending in and am able to relax. Tonight, I feel like a proper part of the family when I am invited inside the hut to watch the new TV. The husband has got his hands on a solar panel which he brought up on the camel. We crowd around the flickering box, an Arabic quiz show, with a donkey. I have no idea what is going on, but it makes me smile and laugh.

Mansour decides to stay up here for a few days, so arranges for his friend to walk me down. En route, we stop with a family whose hut is hidden on a high, exposed ridge. Inside, the atmosphere is nothing like what I have just experienced. The father is cold, with fierce eyes, and his children are withdrawn and wary. As we drink our tea, the boy and girl sit and stare at me. The girl, yet to reach puberty, has her hair wrapped in a frayed blue scarf, and her eyes are wide and afraid. She is vulnerable. This is not a happy family.

I cannot get the image of the girl out of my head. As we move on, we pass groups of playing children who are so unlike her. They look free, while she seemed trapped and broken. I do not know what I can do to help. My guide for the day has disappeared ahead of me, so I push onwards. I reach the top of Wadi Shraig and see his figure far down below me. This valley is steep. The narrow rocky path is made of sharp-edged turns, sided with a vertical drop. It makes me feel dizzy, so I concentrate on the rocks below me, blanking out the drop by my side.

I am overheating, so once I make it down I am relieved to see the man sitting in the shade, next to a deep pool filled by a waterfall pouring through the rocks. I sit and join him, dipping my scarf in the cold water, wrapping it around my hair and neck. He jumps up and continues moving before

I have had time to cool. He does not read me like Mansour does. I sigh and follow him. I do not know this route well and am not happy being here in the shade on my own.

The next few hours are tough. I am hot. Dizzy. I cannot think straight. We arrive in an unfamiliar part of Wadi Itlah, where we stop for a rest with a family for tea. I cannot drink it. The sweet liquid makes me feel nauseous. I am swaying slightly. There are thin hens in a cage beside me that keep squawking. The valley is stretching out beneath us and all I can think of is the final climb. I think it will be impossible.

It is a blur. I did make it out, but now my head is pulsing. The guide has noticed that I am not well and has taken action. He has sat me in the coolest room of his house, next to a small window that is letting in the breeze. I am gulping down icy water, served in a large metal mug, and have splashed it all over my face. My taxi driver Hameed is not home or answering his phone, so I just have to wait here. The guide brings in a big plate of rice, salad and bread, then leaves me in peace, reflecting on the fact that I cannot tolerate the sun as well as he can.

Time passes. I pick at the food, sip at the water, and then stretch out my aching legs. I am beginning to feel a bit stronger, but I am yearning to get back to camp. I need a cold shower and then my bed. There is a small tap at the door. A boy sneaks in, waving at me and grinning. He is ten or so, a beautiful handsome boy, so unlike his father who is wrinkled, with a wavering lazy eye that gazes outwards. I smile back at the boy who runs away, returning with items to dance with. He puts on his coloured hat, digs out his pink feather boa, and begins dancing for me. He sings as he goes, rubbing the boa around his neck and then waving the feathers high above him. He is brilliant, great rhythm and moves. I laugh, leaning back against the wall and enjoying the show. I will get back to camp eventually, and this unexpected wait is worth it.

I do make it back eventually.

The following evening, I am still recovering, lying peacefully in the tent, when I get an unexpected visitor. It is the Japanese woman who I have smiled at and greeted in camp for years, but never spoken to. Tonight, appearing mute, she does not speak but comes and sits by my side. She is wrapped in her thick purple coat, the hood covering up her delicate face and she is clasping a large note pad that I have never seen before. She places it in front of me and starts writing in perfect English, which she knows as well as her own Japanese.

"How are you?" she begins.

I respond happily, telling her about my trip in Wadi Tinya. We chat away, and she keeps her hand in front of her mouth, as if hiding her teeth every time she laughs.

"Will you climb with me to the peak of Mount Katherine?" she writes.

"Oh, it is a beautiful mountain, though a long climb. I have been there twice, and definitely recommend it to you," I reply, and then sit watching her write her response.

"Please come. I need a woman by my side. I am too scared to walk alone with a guide."

She wants to climb tomorrow. I am exhausted, and this is a stranger. I have never exchanged words with her in my life. I cannot do it.

"No. I am too tired to climb. And ever so busy with my work. You should go, though; I can recommend a reputable guide who will keep you safe," I tell her.

She says nothing.

"Okay, well I am going to sleep now. Please let me know if you have any questions. Good night," I finish, standing up and waving goodbye.

She lifts up the paper with one more note.

"Can I have a hug?" she asks.

I feel embarrassed. I do not know this woman. I just laugh and pat her on the shoulder as I leave.

As I lie in bed, I feel shameful. She seems like a kind, sweet person. I should have given her a real, tight hug.

# 2014

*Olivia in the White Canyon, Sinai*

# Chapter 25

It is the dead of night. An old man is pacing aimlessly up and down the road, his eyes out of focus and his mind unaware of where he is going. It is winter, but he is not wearing a coat to fend off the cold. Although he is known to spend time in Fox Camp, he walks straight past this night without giving it a glance, his hunched body looking eerie in the cold light of the electric street lamps. Inside the camp everyone is sleeping, wrapped in thick blankets to try to keep warm. Sophie is the only one who is awake, using the silent hours to hunt. She is now the only cat in camp. Hamza has been sending me regular phone photos of Katkoot, the handsome black and white cat, but Katkoot has disappeared, vanishing just before I arrived back.

It is the last year of my PhD now, and my research has shifted direction. I want to focus on the pollination of the orchard trees, to figure out whether growing flowering herbs in the gardens attracts more pollinators to the trees, or whether it creates competition. The trees flower much earlier in the year, so I am here in February. The sky is still crystal blue by day, but it is cold with an icy breeze. Despite the change in weather and the loss of my favourite cat, I feel like I have arrived home.

It was difficult getting back here. I had to fight even harder with the university for travel permission and was then held at the checkpoint for over an hour. We were forced to drive in a convoy backed by armed police. The intention was to reduce the risk of terrorist attacks, but the line of taxis and coaches filled with tourists made me feel like a target.

My driver, Hameed, got me safely to Fox Camp, where I was greeted with hugs from Hamza, Uncle Omar, and Kareem who is now working here. The camp has changed again. New buildings have popped up for all the tourists who are soon to return. Christine has gone, back to New Zealand with astonishing stories to tell. The Russian nun is still here. As is the silent Japanese girl, still wrapped up tightly in her bright purple coat.

Ben is also in camp. He has written a trekking guidebook about the Sinai, mapping the trails and sharing everything he knows about the mountains and the local culture. Ben and I have crossed paths many times over the years. He used to find Beth and me infuriating. To him, we were giggling girls who took nothing seriously and he had been sure that we would soon rush home to get married and have babies. Now I am here on my own, I seem a little more interesting, someone worth holding a conversation with.

The fact that Ben and I are both English ties us together. We share the same language and culture, so I get filled with delayed festive spirit when he tells me that he has brought over a bottle of mulled wine. Ben suggests an afternoon climb with me, Hamza, Kareem, and Majid, a friendly Egyptian tourist. We decide to follow an unusual route behind the camp, taking us to a small knoll that overlooks the entire village. It is great fun being in the mountains with Hamza, as I have rarely seen him leave the camp. Once the wine has been heated, we take in the views and sip the spiced, warming flavour of home. It feels surreal. I lie with Hamza and Kareem in the sunshine, the cool breeze ruffling my hair and I laugh, thinking how wonderful my life is.

We act like children up there. Hamza and Kareem take hold of my legs and lift me up towards the sun. I stretch my arms as high as I can. Ben is crouched down in front of us, taking photographs of this moment, with the mountains all around us, and Majid gazing up at me and smiling at the friendships he has stumbled across.

As we head back down towards Fox Camp, the photo-shoot becomes more extreme. Ben and Hamza are planning to be snapped in mid-air as they leap across a deep crevice. I raise my safety concerns, but somehow Ben convinces me to be the photographer for the shoot. He has spotted a place down below us, where I can get the perfect view of them framed against the bright blue sky.

I do not know why I have agreed to do this. It is extremely steep, with no established path. I follow Ben slowly and carefully, holding his shoulder each time I slip or stumble, and then I stop. There is a deep drop. I cannot do it. Ben leaps down and reaches his hand up to me. There is a small rock poking out of the boulder, a step. I place my foot on it, take his hand and step down. The rock collapses under my weight and I fall.

My mind goes blank.

I have landed on top of Ben, crushing him flat against the rocks. My body is pressed on top of his, and together we start sliding down, nothing slowing us, down and down and down. I think this is it. The end.

I do not know how far we slide, or how bruised Ben's body is, but eventually we come to a halt. My head is spinning. It takes some time before I realise that I am still alive. I clamber off Ben, slowly moving my shaking limbs and getting to my feet. I see Hamza running towards me, putting his arms around me, guiding me out to easier ground. Behind me Ben has jumped to his feet, uninjured.

"Are you okay?" asks Kareem, scanning my body for injuries.

Majid has gone quiet. They had expected the worse.

I nod and reply, "I am fine."

We begin our walk back down to camp. I am now on a familiar route so feel more comfortable, but the ground is rough and I slip. Kareem turns around, his arm reaching out to catch me. He looks terrified.

"I am okay, don't worry, Kareem," I say with a smile.

It was nothing, just gravel skidding beneath my boots. I am okay. We all make it back to camp. Kareem could not shake off his nervousness and looked round every time my feet crunched on the rocks. He is a small man, no taller than me, and he would not have been able to catch me. I kept thinking of me landing on him, of us tumbling down together, repeating the horrible incident time after time.

"Zanga, zanga. Hara, hara, Bait, bait, number one," Hamza sings, his fingers banging out the now familiar Sa'idi rhythm on the drum, his forefinger swollen and wrapped in a dirty plaster. The rest of us clap along, Kareem pitching in with the lyrics, which we all know and for some reason love.

"No woman no chai, no woman no cry," they sing, Kareem looking right at me from across the fire.

Kareem and I have got closer. I have made it clear that we are nothing but friends, but we are spending far more time together now he works in camp. The friend's boundary was broken briefly last year when he had invited me to climb the small mountain behind camp. It is nicknamed Hamza Mountain, because Hamza tries to encourage every female tourist to climb up there with him for a romantic and private view of the stars.

Kareem and I had climbed up there on my last night in camp. I had known his intentions. I had stood up there and remembered my life in England, where I had no chance of finding a man to kiss! I have a great group of friends at home, with regular pub trips and Chinese takeaways, but I have got far too old for bars and clubs filled with single folk. It had been my last chance of action, so I went for it.

# Chapter 26

Hamza's finger is now red and pulsating, and his hand and arm have started swelling. It is an infection. I have been pushing him to see a doctor, but he just ignores me or shuts me down. As I pack my bag this morning there is no sight of him, so I wander into the kitchen, helping myself to coffee and some of yesterday's stale bread. I set off alone towards the other side of town where I am meeting Mansour at the base of Abu Gifa before today's climb.

As I walk, I notice a man staring at me. I cross the road to keep my distance, looking at my feet and trying to be discreet. The man is a prophet. He stands out, one of the few black men here, who is wearing his familiar dark, embellished galabeya, with reds, blues, greens, and gold around the neck. He has brought his wife and kids to St Katherine from America, to protect them from the apocalypse. On his arrival, he adopted the name Soliman, stocked up the cupboards with tinned food and dug a bunker in the rock below their house. Now he is focused on his spiritual task, rewriting the Koran.

I keep my eyes on the pavement and walk quickly, without looking back. When I reach the base of the mountain, I start scanning the rocks for Mansour. I see his motorcycle parked proudly on the top of a prominent boulder and smile. I continue upwards, feeling relief now that I know Mansour is here. I wind around a corner and find him, crouched down, roll-up in hand. He jumps up and greets me, and on we climb. There has been a seasonal transformation. Many of the trees have shed their greenery over winter, causing the gardens to fade away into the rocky landscape. The almond trees themselves are leafless, covered in pale white buds that are close to opening. For the time being, I am wrapping selected branches in thin netting that will block out the bees and other insects. Later in the year, once the trees have flowered, and those flowers have fruited into young almonds, I will be able to assess how important the pollinators are for producing the almonds and maintaining good yields.

It is an easy and peaceful day up there, but when I get back to camp things are strangely quiet. I wash and wrap up in warm clothes before wandering around camp and searching for people. There is still no sign of Hamza. I bump into Ben, who has not seen him either and together we begin a Hamza hunt. Ben searches the bedroom and finds Hamza curled up and shivering. This is not good. I think the infection has spread into his blood, affecting his entire body. Septicaemia. It could kill him.

I catch sight of Farag pulling into camp in his dark green Land Cruiser and run to get his help.

"Farag, Hamza is sick. He cannot walk. He needs to go to hospital now," I plead.

"Ha ha," Farag chuckles fondly. "Hamza is strong, he does not need the doctors. He is Sa'idi," he says insistently.

Hamza is not strong; he is weak and I fear he may be dying. I search camp, and urge Kareem, Uncle Omar and everyone else I can find to take action, but they are all united: he is Sa'idi, he is strong. I am making a fuss.

There is a genuine dislike of Sa'idi people here. Hamza is the only one working with the tourists, with the rest of the Sa'idi men heaving rocks and constructing the new buildings across camp. Hamza is strong, but is thinner and paler than the other Sa'idi's, passing as a Bedouin at first glance. He is valued by Farag and the other staff members, but they still view him as different, as an outsider.

The sun is setting and Hamza is still alone, unable to stand or move. Ben and I continued pressing for Hamza to be given medical attention, but everyone dismissed us, repeatedly insisting that he was Sa'idi and strong. I am sure they would not treat him like this if he was family. I tried to explain the condition of septicaemia multiple times, but no-one understood me. They lacked the basic biological knowledge of our bodies, they did not know we were made of cells, or what bacteria are, and it was too hard to teach them everything. I know that Hamza at times appears a creepy and untrustworthy man, and that he once tried to sexually abuse me when I was drunk, but he deserves to live.

I sit down on the steps by my room and place my head in my hands. Then an idea comes to me. I call Ben over and start rummaging through my first aid kit. I find what I am looking for.

"Ben, antibiotics are what we need right?" I ask him, handing him the crumpled packet of tablets.

He reads the details and nods.

"Yes, these should work," he replies.

Ben's father is a doctor, as is mine, and I feel relieved that he agrees with my prescription.

Ben takes the packet to Hamza and watches him swallow the first tablet. It works. By morning, Hamza is up, drowsy but able to eat and talk. Those tablets have been in my bag for years, packed to treat a bad case of the squits. They are probably past their best by date, but they have done the job and Hamza is back with us.

Hamza crashes again that evening, disappearing back inside himself. Despite our medical families, Ben and I are not cut out for prescribing drugs. We had not given him a high enough daily dose. Luckily we notice the crash. Internet searches and a phone call with my dad set us back on track and with the correct dosage, Hamza's body fights the infection. Within a couple of days, he is out of bed and back at work. He has won the fight.

Al'Hamd'Allah. Thanks be to God.

# Chapter 27

Things are looking up. Hamza is well, the almonds are blossoming and, more importantly, Sean is back! I have convinced him to spend the next two months working as my field assistant. He is an extraordinary ecologist and a brilliant friend, so I am excited about having his help and his company. He arrived this evening and having him join us in the tent feels like a real treat. Sophie climbs all over him as Hamza pours the tea and I chat away, sharing all the gossip. It ranges from the grim death of Katkoot, whose body I recently saw by the side of the road, through to the miraculous survival of Hamza. I tell him about last year's floods and how bare the mountains look in winter, and he fills me in on life at home. I could talk all night, but Sean looks tired from his long day of travel, so we say good night. I am so looking forward to working with him.

The plan is for Sean to help me with the almond surveys, but he has also inspired me to look at the birds. He is an excellent birder and I could not do this without him as he can spot and identify tiny song birds hidden within a tree canopy, birds which are entirely invisible to me. After a day of rest, Sean and I head to Wadi Itlah to begin surveying the flowering trees.

"Sean! Welcome back," calls Mansour, smiling and shaking Sean's hand when we arrive.

"Sure, it is great to be back," replies Sean in his lilting Irish accent.

We cross down into the valley and are greeted by an unmatchable view. The almond trees have come into bloom and pale pink clouds of blossom are now floating down the valley. The gardens, which are usually green and impressive, have now become dreamlike, with delicate white flowers bursting over their walls. Up close, the blossoms give off a sweet scent and there is a low hum from the huge numbers of honeybees feasting on the nectar and pollen. We spend the morning observing the other insects visiting the flowers, the smaller wild bees and the astonishing large, hairy beetles which are swathed in pollen. Sean and I laugh and chat as we go, Sean armed with his binoculars at all times and shrieking at the sight of a Sinai Rose Finch or the luck-bringing Bhagar.

Mansour cooks us a special lunch today—fresh baba ganoush from aubergines roasted on the open fire. After eating, Mansour and I sigh and lie back, both opting for sheltered sun traps that protect us from the winter breeze. I nap happily, feeling the sun's rays illuminating my face and warming my body. Sean is too restless to nap. He leaves us there, exploring the wadi, climbing the valley sides, peering into the nooks and crannies, armed with his binoculars and his new GoPro video camera.

In the evening, cheap whiskey is whipped out. Everyone is crowded around the fire, each wrapped in a thick blanket to fend off the cold. Hamza pours out glasses of whiskey and coke, grinning as he passes them round. Uncle Omar tuts heavily, and sits back lighting his cigarette, but Sean and I accept the drinks gladly. Kareem sits close to me, our legs nestled together beneath the blankets. I offer him my glass and he takes a sip. He would not share with anyone else, but things have moved on between us. You might say that we are an item.

It is a secret. Hamza and Ben know, having observed our interactions and changes in behaviour, but I cannot bring myself to reveal it to Sean. It is silly. Last year I was infatuated with Kareem's younger brother, who outperforms him in terms of sexiness, but Kareem's intelligence, wit and persistence have won me round. It started a week ago, a drunken evening ending in my bed. Since then we have been inseparable during the nights. Kareem's red sleeping bag has moved in to my room, and in combination with his body heat and additional blankets, I am now able to keep cosy and warm.

Kareem has been here since my last visit, choosing not to return home to his life in Slovenia. He still messages his wife and daughter, sending dozens of heart and smiley face emojis, but he rarely speaks to them and does not seem to have the intention of going home. I do feel guilty, but Kareem and his wife seem to have separated, and his family life seems like something from a distant world.

Kareem knows that he is misbehaving, and it is niggling him. He is the one who insists on secrecy, because he dreads the thought of his village finding out what he is up to. Prayer helps to clear his mind and his conscience. He is a spiritual man, and prays regularly in the new mosque that has been constructed in camp. He uses the time to appeal for forgiveness and it helps, calming him and giving him temporary relief from his guilt.

It is wonderful spending so much time with Sean. Our days are now filled by surveys of the birds as well as the almond pollinators. He has opened my eyes to the small migratory birds that are feasting on insects within the flowering trees. The treecreeper climbing slowly up a gnarled old tree, and partridges scurrying across the rocks and keeping their distance from the gardens. The most impressive sight was the raptors. We caught sight of them midway on their migration, thirty or more birds of prey, gliding slowly together through the centre of the wadi. Astonishing.

In camp, Sean and I spend a lot of time together, but my situation with Kareem makes things awkward. Kareem will often jump away from me if Sean approaches, and I am always shuffling, not able to be open and myself. Sean knows that something is going on. He has noticed how in camp I become shy, shifty, giggly, and confusing. It puzzles him.

It is late afternoon when Sean knocks on my bedroom door, hoping to hang out, to chat and watch TV repeats on my laptop. Behind him cracked wooden boards lean against the wall, my old bed waiting to be disposed of. I welcome him in and we both sit down on my mattress, which is now lying on the concrete floor. Sean does not know how my bed frame broke. I could not tell him that the boards had cracked during aerobic activity between Kareem and myself. Luckily he did not hear us giggling quietly in the dark that night. The beds are cheaply made and not high quality, so Sean did not question it. But Hamza knew exactly who and what were the cause of the breakage.

Sean and I sit down on the mattress, with the electric fire turned on radiating gentle heat in our direction. Before I turn the laptop on, I have something to say.

"Sean, I have something that I need to tell you," I say, catching his eye briefly, before looking at my lap.

Sean laughs nervously, his mind racing. He was not expecting this, but he knew something was up. Am I okay? Has something bad happened? Oh man, perhaps his girlfriend was right. Do I fancy him? Am I about to declare my love?

"Kareem and I, are, um, sort of together," I say, interrupting Sean's thoughts. "I am sorry I didn't tell you earlier. Kareem is being really secretive, but I just wanted you to know, so that I don't have to hide anything from you."

"Woah. I had no idea," Sean says, letting out his breath. This is easier to deal with than a love declaration.

"Good on you both. You need to enjoy yourself while you're here," he says, smiling. "Kareem is a lucky man."

## Chapter 28

The weather has changed. The clear blue sky has faded white through to grey. It is not a day for working. Instead, Sean and I head out for a stroll with a young Irishman staying in camp, who is nicknamed Moustafa. He has spent a lot of time here, a good friend of Kareem, with a deep knowledge of the people and the place. As we walk, he tells us a story, a tale about the cave of the grave of the ogress.

The fierce ogress had lived alone in Wadi Itlah, creeping around in the shadows high up on the mountainside. When she died, the rocks had cracked open around her, creating a cave for her grave, a cave filled with darkness and doom. It is a silly story, but as we are told it in the cold icy wind, I feel a shiver down my spine. When we reach the base of Wadi Itlah the sky has darkened. I have walked here countless times, but I have never noticed the cave. Moustafa points up at the gaping holes, before turning back and wishing us luck with our exploration.

There it is, the cave of the grave of the ogress. It is situated up on the right side of the valley. The deep cave and cracks appear to take the form of the ogress herself. There is an enormous, cavernous mouth, and above it a misshapen nose and two ferocious cracked eyes. Sean wants to get closer. I follow Sean off the path, the two of us scrambling our way towards the cave. I stop when we reach the cave's entrance, but Sean is keen to get footage within the engulfing blackness. I tell him I will wait outside and then watch him disappear, his footsteps echoing as he goes deeper into the cave.

Time goes slowly out here. Light snowflakes begin to fall. I look down the slope and feel giddy. I have to shift my weight to keep myself steady. The gravelly rock slips beneath me and I am falling all over again. I cannot think straight, my heart is beating uncontrollably. Within moments, Sean is by my side, coming as soon as he heard my scream. He jumped from rock to rock, without any of my fear, and now he is talking to me reassuringly, saying that everything will be okay.

Sean takes my hand and leads me down to the flatter rocks, speaking calming words as we go. As soon as I am away from the slope, which had looked so steep, I calm down and then begin to feel embarrassed. My fear disappeared as soon as I made it away from the steep slope. It is as if I have developed a weird vertigo, or perhaps it is just panic, a result of the fall with Ben. I need to get a grip, to train my racing mind to slow down and not scream every time I come across a slippery slope.

Sean distracts me as we walk, telling me all about the engulfing darkness of the cave, the towering height and the vibrating echoes. It sounds impressive, the only problem being that he did not spot the body of the ogress.

When we make it back to camp it is cold. The gentle snow has not settled but the sky has continued to darken. Sean and I wrap ourselves in blankets and drink cup after cup of tea. By late afternoon we are both ready to move again. We decide to join a tourist who is walking up Wadi Shraig. We climb up to my favourite point, where the view of the camp and the road disappear. Above us, long black clouds stretch heavily across the mottled sky, and below us the mountains are wrapped in white cloud. It is as if we are floating. Sean and I head back, but the man we are with tells us that he is going to continue upwards until he makes it to the top of Gebel Musa. He is the son of a high-ranking Egyptian police officer, a father who sounds determined and powerful. The son seems the same and, despite our warnings, he continues climbing confidently, waving goodbye as we disappear into the mist.

At the same time, eight friends nearby are feasting upon chicken and marvelling at the clouds rolling across the sky. They came down from Cairo to climb Gebel Baab il Donya and found a young guide who has let them climb despite the icy weather. Farag had offered them a well-trained guide but they had found this boy in the village. He had offered to lead them for a much cheaper price. By the time they pack up their food, the snow has started falling heavily. It is too late to climb back down and the guide becomes confused and scared.

It is a blizzard. Things spiral out of control. The snow quickly becomes fast and heavy up there on the mountain peaks. Everything is white. There is no visibility. The guide does not know where to go, but the group of young Egyptian friends are all following him hopefully, all hunched up and pushing through the snow. There is a hut, with piles of firewood just one hundred metres from where they walk, but it is invisible and their guide does not know that it exists.

One girl from the group is shivering uncontrollably. She feels that she cannot go on. She stops, tears dripping from her eyes, and falls to her knees, her hands sinking into the inches of powdery snow. The friends group together, shouting to one another over the unbearable wind. They are all panicking. They do not know what to do. One lays his hands on the back of the kneeling girl.

"Stay here, you are too tired to walk on. When we find safety, we will come back for you," he says to her in Arabic.

She nods silently and watches them disappear into the snow.

The group pushes on through the wind and snow, led by the young boy who they have no choice but to follow. They walk for an hour. Everyone's muscles beginning to stiffen, noses and fingers going numb. Then they see something in the distance, bright green. One of them calls and begins running.

It is her. The girl is motionless, her green coat and colourful headscarf standing out against the white snow. The cold has been too much for her, far worse because she was still and motionless. They had left their friend alone, gripped by fear, with nobody there to hold her as she weakened. She is dead. One of the men starts to cry. His friend puts his arm around his shoulders, while another bends down to embrace the stiff, cold body. The whole group is overcome with grief, but panic is beginning to creep in about their own fates.

They are lost, their guide has walked them in a circle. One of the young men starts scrabbling in his pocket and pulls out a lighter with the hope of making fire. He digs around in the snow and grabs a handful of wet twigs which he tries desperately to light. It is impossible, the wind knocking out the flame time after time. They cannot make fire so they must move on, it is too cold to stay put. As they look around the vast whiteness they see that their guide has gone.

He has fled. He knows that he should not have but he was scared for his life and was certain that he had a stronger chance of finding his way home without them. So the friends walk forwards into the unknown, leaving the dead body behind them.

## Chapter 29

Up above there is a deep rumble from the black, military helicopter passing overhead. The helicopters have been circling slowly around the snow-capped mountains all morning, searching in vain for the group of Egyptians and their deceased friend. The young guide made it down to his family yesterday, with frostbite to both his fingers and toes. He was in a bad way but had put out the alert and the helicopters were brought in immediately. The dead girl's parents were also phoned as a priority and they drove straight here, the two of them now sitting hopelessly as they wait for their child's body to be found.

The weather down at the camp has stilled, but the snow continues up in the high mountains, where the falling flakes are disrupting visibility from the helicopters. It is making the search near impossible. It is too cold to work, so Sean and I are sitting and waiting for news. Everyone is gathered in the office for a bit of warmth, with talk circulating about the incident. People are angry with the guide for abandoning his tourists. Most people seem to know the precise location of the nearby hut that would have protected the group, offering shelter and firewood. It is shameful, his lack of knowledge and experience are what had caused the death. A tragedy.

The day drags by. There is an ongoing drone of helicopters in the background and the atmosphere in camp is morose. On the positive side, the man we climbed with yesterday made it back safely. He had walked quickly, finding the established trail to the summit. Although a few flakes dusted the ground around him, he had made it down before the real snow began. I am relieved that he is alright, but I cannot shake the thought of the group who are still up there.

I struggle to sleep at night. When the sky darkened, the helicopters landed with no news of success, and everything has been put on pause until the morning. Now Kareem and I are lying together, fully dressed, buried in blankets and his sleeping bag. The electric heater is whirring away, and I have wrapped my arms and legs around him to share our body heat. We are warm and safe, but my mind keeps returning to the friends spending their second night up there, utterly lost and surrounded by snow.

By morning nothing has changed. The helicopters were back in the air at first light and people are still worried. Hamza is getting particularly agitated about the dead girl.

"She needs to be buried," he says to me as I am eating breakfast. He is pacing about, furious that the helicopters have failed to find the body.

"She deserves to be buried as soon as possible; we need to stick to the true Islamic way," he intones.

I have never seen Hamza so stirred up by his religion. Last year, when I was present for the early days of Ramadan, he spent his time breaking the rules by drinking black coffee and smoking during the daylight hours, and I never see him go to prayer.

Despite Hamza's casual attitude towards religion, I know that he has a deep belief in his god, Allah. Many years ago, we had an in-depth discussion in which he tried to prove the undeniable existence of God. How else could you explain why the sun and moon circle through the sky, or why a rock always falls downwards to the floor if you drop it, or why big chunks of wood float on water instead of sinking. He is an intelligent, although uneducated man, and I answered all his well thought through questions with science, explaining about orbits, gravity, and density. Hamza had not heard of any of these theories, and I did nothing to shake him from his belief.

By late afternoon Hamza is going mad. There is still no news about the rescue mission, so he has decided to climb up there himself. He will carry down her body and ensure that it gets buried as soon as possible, thus avoiding another sunset lying unprotected in the snow. He approaches everyone who passes through camp, trying to recruit them on his mission. They all turn him down, warning him about the risks of the ongoing blizzard. They are right. Hamza is dressed in nothing but his jeans and a cheap, brown coat. He would not last a minute up there.

The helicopters continue searching for another two days. They have found the living members of the group, who have been successfully guided down to safety. They had located some shelter, which had protected them from the fierce wind overnight, but it did not save all of them. Another three are dead. The four dead bodies have remained there for three bleak nights, with the army unable to land their helicopters on the uneven, snow-covered rocks. It is a horrendous tragedy.

The snow begins to melt, and the bodies are finally rescued. In camp, the sadness begins to fade, but the friends who were up there will never forget what has happened to them and nor will the families of the deceased. Within the valleys, the snow melt has started running with an innocent purity, forming streams and pools alongside the flowering trees. Sean and I return to work. Where we are, you cannot see the damage that the storms have caused. Instead, the wadis are shimmering with life, bees covering the blossoms and birds flitting between the trees.

Mansour talks about the event, deeply saddened by the deaths that should never have happened. He tells us of the time he was trapped in a snowstorm. He had noticed the weather changing before the snow began to fall, and had steered his tourists towards a cave. They had stayed there for a day and a night, safe by the fire, happy and laughing at the strange circumstances that they found themselves in. I am beginning to realise the danger of these mountains, and how shielded I am by working with Mansour, a man who is so connected to the terrain, the weather and the people.

# *Chapter 30*

Sean feels great in Sinai. At home, he often feels flat, but here the vitality of the wadis blows all that away. He is looking forward to sharing it with Siobhan, his girlfriend, who is visiting soon. The sky is blue again, the white sun shining brightly and he is filled with optimism. She will love the blossom-filled valleys and the rolling sand dunes. Her trip will finish with pure relaxation by the sea.

Before Siobhan arrives, there is the rugby to enjoy. The Six Nations are in battle and today it is England versus Ireland, Sean versus me. Of course, we are unable to watch the match live at Twickenham, and we are lacking pubs with large screens here in Sinai. However, Sean has found an Irish radio station that is streaming the match. The two of us are sitting on the terrace, phone in the centre of the table and both of us are excited. Kareem has no interest and has wandered off into the kitchen, but Hamza is watching curiously from a seat in the corner.

The match begins, but I am struggling to visualise what is happening. I always watch rugby live or on the tv-screen, and the radio voices sound disjointed and far away. Sean has a solution. He turns the table into the pitch, with the salt and pepper pots becoming the players. He moves them around in response to the radio presenters, bringing the game to life. It is brilliant, and has the two of us laughing together, in between our rival gasps and sighs. It is a tense match with England the victors, winning 13–10! A great match.

We are unable to move on to a pub to celebrate, or commiserate, Instead, we simply adjourn to the tent and drink tea. It has been surreal watching rugby here on the Fox Camp tabletop.

Later that afternoon, Sean goes for his usual bird-watching wander in the olive garden, and Kareem joins me in the tent, lying his head against my leg. He browses on his phone, as I run my fingers through his hair, twizzling his thick curls. I had a recent experience of hair styling, modelling Kareem on Sophie when her fur was looking particularly scruffy and matted. I spent over an hour putting little plaits amongst all his curls, creating an uncanny similarity between him and cat.

Kareem is surprisingly tolerant of my hair grooming behaviour. Human touch can often make him uncomfortable since he is anxious about the spreading of unwanted dirt. He is revolted by cigarette smoke and must rewash a teacup before accepting an offered drink. In our bedroom, he refuses to place his head on the poorly laundered pillow case, insisting that we lay his own T-shirt across the pillow before we sleep. This does mean that seams or buttons from his clothing tend to dig into my cheek, but I tolerate it just to reduce his stress. He also needs his sleeping bag because he knows the blankets are ingrained with fire smoke. That does not bother me so much during these cold nights.

Our blankets and sleeping bags become more important in the coming week, as the sky darkens once again. When Siobhan arrives, the clouds are heavy and ready to burst. Sean is delighted to see her, but he is gutted that the world he had hoped to share with her has darkened. Siobhan herself is feeling down, just learning about her grandfather's death and the black skies seem to mirror her mood.

I wake early morning to the sound of heavy rain. There is no sight of Kareem next to me, so I close my eyes and listen to the incessant thudding on the roof. After I had dozed for a while, Kareem returns, bursting through the door. His long hair is flattened, soaked with the rain and his face is lit by an unmatchable smile. I jump up and sit next to him on the tent's other, unbroken, bed that doubles as a seat, and he shows me his photos. He has run up Wadi Shraig, jumping across the high rocks, and videoing the river of water that has now taken over the valley.

Kareem and I head out into the storm. I spin around in the heavy droplets and Kareem smiles at the life-giving water falling from the sky. He climbs on a wall in the olive garden, strong brown currents running behind him. He puts his hands high in the sky and sings, "Rain, rain, rain." The water falls into his mouth and the two of us laugh with joy.

The two of us then walk over to the main road, where the water is now deep and aggressive. It reaches our ankles and in places comes over our knees. The cars can hardly drive, and a gathering of people stand by the side of the road watching their attempts. After splashing and laughing, the two of us retreat to our room, slowly removing our dripping jumpers and jeans. We crawl into our bed, wrapping ourselves up and kissing each other until we are dry. We spend the day there, exploring each other's bodies, cocooned from the outside world.

Next door, Sean and Siobhan are lying together in silence. They have not been out to explore, instead feeling blocked in and trapped. Sean feels anxious, unsure what to do to make Siobhan happy. She is grieving, tears dripping down her face as the rain crashes above them. The following day things have settled, but the grey sky is still heavy above us. People emerge from their rooms. We use the office to reconnect with one another as we wait for the tent cushions to dry.

Kareem is intrigued by Sean and Siobhan's relationship, watching their every move. He knows nothing about her personal troubles and is shocked by the care and attention that Siobhan is receiving. Sean is acting as a host, making sure that Siobhan has everything she needs. When we sit in the once-again habitable tent, Siobhan makes a firm request for a jumper, and Sean leaps to his feet, running to their room to retrieve it. Kareem smirks. He would never consider fetching items for me, and nor would I for him.

Siobhan's Sinai experience starts to improve. The skies are clearing and the three of us head out to Wadi Itlah. There are now rivers of silver running down the sandy valley, framed either side by the blossoming trees. Mansour feeds us wonderful food, and Siobhan's tense shoulders begin to relax as she sips his soothing tea. Sean scores even higher marks for his hosting skills when we go out to the low desert. Qasim drives us in his familiar white Land Cruiser, Bob Marley blaring from the speakers. He takes us to the idyllic sand dunes, with miles of rolling white sand, the grains so fine that they run easily through your fingertips. Qasim has brought sand-boards, which Sean, Siobhan and I attach to our feet, giving us the chance to slowly surf down the soft sand.

Qasim watches us from the bottom of the dune, laughing as we slide our way down. I go and join him, cracking open the beer he hands me. Sean and Siobhan are more adventurous than me, investigating the rocks at the top of the dune, while I stretch out my legs and soak up the winter sun. I look at the tall and handsome, married man who is sitting companionably by my side and smile, tipping my head back to gaze at the vivid blue sky.

The serenity of the sand dunes does not last long. Qasim is ready to show off his driving skills, so beckons us all back into the Land Cruiser. He takes us deeper into the desert, with tall white dunes on either side. Sean has attached his GoPro video camera to the wing mirror, so that it captures our drive across the rippled sand. We pause at the edge of a deep dune, taking in the view, before Qasim puts his foot down. We fly down the edge of the dune, my stomach flipping as if I am on a roller coaster. Then we go up and over, gliding down the next dune.

Qasim is an astonishing driver. A few years ago, he received a phone call from people stuck in the desert. He diverted from our planned route, driving us out there to assist. On arrival, we found two macho Egyptian men and a local Bedouin guide who had driven their four-by-four over one of the deepest dunes and had got stuck, unable to make their way up and over the other side of the dune. Qasim worked for an hour trying to help, adding rocks beneath the tyres to increase the grip but the car would still not come out. In the end, we had to leave them with a bottle of water and a packet of biscuits. As we drove away, the Bedouin man looked at us with sadness, knowing that it was going to be a long wait before they were rescued.

Qasim and Farag had driven back the following day, needing multiple vehicles to drag out the stranded car and rescue the men. Here, tribal connections are what you need in the case of an emergency, and Qasim is the man to call when your car is stuck in the desert.

Today, Qasim is trying to show off his driving skills. He is not aiming to impress me, his ex-lover, but is focused on the GoPro, hoping that it will record his unequalled sand-duning abilities. He takes us to an even higher dune, one that he avoids with other tourists. We plunge over the summit, but fail to make it over the opposite side, instead curving round to the left with the Land Cruiser tilting precariously inwards before coming to a halt.

"You need to get out," he tells us in a serious voice.

He wants to lighten the load in the vehicle to increase the chance of making it over and out. We begin climbing up the dune to clear his way. It is a slow climb, with my feet sinking into the deep sand. From the top we watch the car circle around and around, occasionally nearing the top, but failing every time.

The view from up here is breath-taking and Sean walks around capturing the scenes on his camera. I sit down on the sand next to Siobhan, clasping my knees. I look at my phone and see that there is no signal. I remember the path we drove up and wonder whether we should start walking back, covering our heads, taking all our water, and simply hoping for the best.

# *Chapter 31*

Qasim did make it out of the sand dune trap. It took a good hour of intense driving in circles, but he got us all home in one piece. Sean and Siobhan are now heading to Dahab for a much-deserved break. Sean is keen to snorkel amongst the coral reefs and explore the marine life of the Red Sea. He has never done it before having previously had a fear of swimming, but it lifted recently. I am the opposite. I used to snorkel happily until I encountered the jelly fish that filled me with panic and fear. Now I prefer swimming in the deep water, keeping my head in the fresh air, blocking out thoughts of what could be lurking below me.

I go down to Dahab and join them to watch the last round of the Six Nations. The three of us find ourselves entirely alone in a bar that is streaming Ireland versus France. Ireland smash it, winning the game and pipping England to the Championship title. It is great fun watching them claim the glory they deserve. I am never sure about sport and the way it engenders competitive hate between the fans of opposing teams. But here we are celebrating together, and I am delighted to see my friends celebrate their team's win.

After the sea break, Siobhan flies back home leaving us to readjust to our Fox Camp normal. Out in the wadis the water is still running, and the trees are now producing leaf, restoring the life in the gardens, and showing that spring is on its way. In the evenings, we still gather in the tent, taking advantage of the warming weather. By night Kareem and I are always together.

Kareem and I have tended to avoid physical contact in public, but now we openly snuggle together in the tent. We often get confused looks from tourists, who are astonished to see the connections between me and a man from this strange Bedouin tribe. Their looks make me smile and feel proud of what the two of us have. I know that it is limited, confined to this camp and the culture within it. Though it is all light-hearted, I am beginning to care for him.

Kareem and I are not in a serious relationship. He flirts with other women, particularly with Marie, a lady from France. I once caught him in the staff bedroom on his smart phone having a bit of fun with her. I was furious, stopping him immediately, yet somehow it did not matter. I ended up laughing at what an idiot he is and let it go. We will never stay together, and this is just about companionship and fun.

Tonight, I am curled up in bed when Kareem comes in and begins undressing. He is taking off his jacket when his phone bleeps.

"My stepdad is dead," he reads aloud in an unusual voice.

I think he is joking and let out a little laugh. He looks at me and I see that this is serious.

"I have to go to my family," he says, pain now creeping into his voice.

He puts his arms back into his jacket, and then he is gone.

I do not see him for days. I lie there each night alone, thinking about him and what he is feeling. I feel so helpless. I want to hold him, stroke his hair, and try to share his pain.

I look at my phone and decide to send a message.

"I hope you are coping OK. I am here when you need me. I love you."

Message sent. Kareem views the message almost immediately, but I do not get a response.

Kareem, Jamal and Soliman, the three brothers, have all attended the funeral and are spending time looking after their mother. She is grieving heavily and is alone, left to care for their younger half-brother. When Kareem comes back to camp he seems empty and disengaged. He will not talk to me, avoiding our room at night and hardly looking at me.

I am sitting in the tent when Kareem finally approaches me. I quickly put out the cigarette that I know he hates.

"Kareem, how are you?" I ask him.

He says nothing but comes and lies down next to me, placing his head in my lap. He starts to weep. His body shakes and shudders, and I hold him close to me, trying to absorb some of his grief. I thought that I had helped but that night Kareem still avoids our room, instead sleeping alone in the shabby staff bedroom. I know things are difficult for him— his grief is more important than my sleeping habits—but I feel frustrated. I want to be there for him. I want to help.

The next evening Uncle Omar comes and sits beside me, the fire crackling in front of us. He has observed that my mood has changed, and he knows what is wrong with me. The two of us tend to laugh and joke in Arabic, talking little sense but becoming true friends. Tonight, he speaks in slow English, explaining the situation and what is going on.

"Kareem has lost his father," he begins.

I nod in acknowledgement, feeling flat.

"Islamic rule is that he cannot sleep with woman for one month after the death," he follows. "He likes you, but he must follow rule."

"Oh, I had no idea," I reply.

It makes more sense now; I see why he is avoiding our room.

Uncle Omar places his hand on mine to comfort me, and I thank him for helping me understand what is going on. Then, the old man leans forward and tries to kiss me on the lips! With my hand still in his, I swerve out the way, leaping to my feet and running from the tent.

"Thank you for telling me, but I do not want any kisses!" I call as I run off towards my room.

I wish Kareem had told me this. I now have greater respect for his actions and feel less troubled that my accidental inclusion of the words "I love you" in my message had made him run a mile. I do not love him, but I do care for him. I want to hold him and help him cope with his grief. I am leaving within the month, so we will never spend another night together.

# 2015

*Camels in South Sinai*

# Chapter 32

It is spring the following year and I am back.

I had settled in quickly at home, writing my PhD thesis and publishing in scientific journals. I know that some people find their PhD stressful and emotional, but I have loved the whole process. There was Sinai, but there was also Nottingham where I spent so much time with other PhD students and friends. We have learnt so much from one another, sharing ideas in our office, and regularly attending the local pub quiz—which we never won. In between socialising, I spent hours crafting my thesis and explaining the way in which the gardens here can benefit nature.

While I was writing, I always thought of the mountains and never felt too far away, but the person who has drawn me back is Kareem. He has been sending me messages throughout the year, silly, romantic chat which I suspect he is sharing with other women. The messages did keep him in my thoughts though, making it hard to forget the closeness that we had built. I handed in my PhD thesis in January and am still waiting for my viva, the interview that will determine if I pass or fail. I have time to fill, so I decided to come back and resolve the mystery of Kareem, the man who I cannot shake from my mind.

Although it was early morning and dark when I arrived, I can see that all has changed. A stone wall is being built around the camp, a barrier to keep people out, and there is a new large tent in the carpark facing the road. Inside the camp, there is still the neon F.O.X. sign propped up on

Hamza mountain, but beneath it there is now a hand-built waterfall, trickling down into a pond inhabited by farm-yard ducks. It is bizarre, seeing water sparkling and mallards quacking, here in the desert. Farag is always building and expanding, but none of this feels right.

Over breakfast, I learn about the new situation. The camp is under new management once again. It is being rented by Rasheed, a rich Emirati man and his wife. Rasheed moved here a few years ago, transforming a garden at the base of Wadi Shraig into what he calls an organic farm. He has paid Bedouin like Jamal to do the work, while he sits around enjoying the view. He is a hippy of sorts, with long grey hair and a tendency to laugh. In the past, I have often spent time with him, sharing jokes with sex-obsessed Christine, eating a delicious stuffed pigeon at the start of Ramadan, and drinking plenty of tea.

Today, I walk into the office to introduce myself to his wife, who I have heard very little about. Her name is Suzy, and she comes from London. She tells me that she is a nu-merologist and I am impressed. I respond with my own ex-perience of statistics but realise I have made a mistake. Nu-merology allocates numbers to aspects of life and uses them to predict the future. It overlaps little with science. It seems that the primary goal of Rasheed and Suzy is to convert Fox Camp into a more spiritual place, designed for yoga retreats and pure relaxation.

Kareem and Hamza are not here. Hamza has gone back to Luxor, where he will spend several months with his family. He does this regularly and, when he is away, I always feel concerned for his wife. He has told me explicitly that her use is for sex, criticising her performance and telling me how she must remove all her bodily hair. Every time he returns here, she seems to have fallen pregnant, being left alone to provide all the care.

I ring Kareem to see where he is. He comes and meets me in the carpark but refuses to come in. He begins pacing backwards and forwards. He is furious. Suzy has banned him from camp. Last week he was seen causing trouble with his tourists, allowing drinking, and flirting that were no longer acceptable under the new camp regime. Kareem had done nothing wrong, so he was not going to apologise or ask for her forgiveness.

Kareem had stopped working in camp when Suzy arrived, so now he is working with tourists as a mountain guide. This is good for him but means he is not able to spend time with me, even though I have travelled all this way to see him. He tells me all of this out here in the carpark, where we are on display. He did shake my hand in greeting but we cannot hug or kiss. He will not come into the camp for a cup of tea, so we simply say goodbye.

I do not know what I will do now. Kareem had known when I was coming, and I had naively thought that he would spend his time with me. Instead, he will not enter camp and has just told me that he will be away for the next three days leading a tourist trail. There are very few people in camp and on my first night the tent is empty. It turns out that Bedouin men from the village, many of whom are my friends, are no longer allowed in camp. If they are here with tourists, they must sit in the new carpark tent, giving the tourists a private fireside experience. The new management considered it a waste of money to provide the Bedouin with free tea and firewood, so now they can make their own in the large, draughty tent outside.

I cannot relax. I already feel like I do not belong here. I go for a stroll around the camp's olive grove, which is filled with so many memories, before being drawn up to Wadi Shraig. I keep on walking, feeling a sense of relief about being back in the mountains that are still my own. I climb past my favourite garden, moving up the less familiar path. I walked this route so many times searching for lizards, but it was a long time ago. I do not know if I will remember the way and I am all alone, wearing cheap trainers and have not brought water. Despite all this, I keep on climbing.

I have never walked on my own, always walking with friends or a guide who can catch me if I fall. It is making me a bit nervous, but my irritation about the changes in camp are pushing me on. I make it into the wide valley, feeling calmer as the wind blows in my hair and the route comes back to me. I follow the path round to Wadi Arbien, heading down the more familiar route to the road.

I did it. I feel a little elated. I make it back to camp for lunch, where I bump into someone I know at last. It is Ben. I tell him about my independent walk. Ben knows these mountains like the back of his hand and is surprised that I went out alone. I have rarely spent much time alone with Ben, but by evening we decide to eat together in town, avoiding the flat vibe in the camp. While we are out, Ben invites me to test out a new mountain challenge route that he is developing. He wants to check that the route is manageable, and will not cause problems for the less athletic trekkers.

Since Kareem is too busy to spend time with me, it is great to have someone to walk with. I set out with Ben and an older Austrian man, Leo, who he has also recruited for the task. We spend a great day clambering up rocks. I am given a piece of rope to haul myself up and am able to do it, with the guys there to give me a hand. Once finished, Ben invites Leo and me to join him on the new Three Peaks Challenge, climbing to the top of Jebel Abbas Basha, then Mount Katherine and ending at Mount Sinai. The walk will continue throughout the night and will be guided by Abdul. Yes, the Abdul who tried to attack Beth. Ben knows about this incident but has continued to work closely with Abdul over the years. I am still extremely wary of the man but, in Ben's eyes, he is loyal and trustworthy and knows every crevice of the mountains that Ben is mapping.

I agreed to join them on the trip later in the week. I know that Ben and Leo's company will keep me safe, and it is great to have something to fill my time even though the thought of walking with Abdul has made me uncomfortable. I remember my distress when I received Beth's phone call, and listened to her fleeing down the mountain. I cannot imagine how she had felt. It must never happen again to anyone. I decide to tell Suzy, so she knows that he cannot be trusted to guide lone women. I walk into the office, where she is standing behind the desk. She looks up at me and I blurt it all out.

"Suzy, I just wanted to talk to you about the guide Abdul. I do not know if you have heard what happened to my friend. She worked alone up in the mountains with him. One night there was an episode when he tried to rape and attack her," I say quickly and then pause.

"I just wanted you to know, so that you never allocate Abdul as a guide for a small group of women sleeping on the mountains. It is not safe. It must never happen again," I finish and look at her for a response.

She chuckles. "I know all about the guides, and I am able to make my own decisions on these matters," she replies, her voice sounding overconfident and cocky.

She says nothing else and begins writing in the office book, so I leave feeling deflated and ignored.

Before I spend time in the presence of Abdul, I am going on a two-night trip with Kareem. It will not be the two of us alone on a romantic getaway. Instead, I am to be a gate crasher. Kareem is the guide, taking a group of tourists on a trip to the Eco Lodge at El-Kalm, and I am allowed to tag along. We start off in Wadi Itlah, where I introduce myself to the rest of the group. We set off and I walk by Kareem's side, the two of us laughing and joking together as we pass through the familiar landscape. Behind us the tourists gaze at the gardens and clamber over the rocks, catching us up when Kareem crouches down to make tea.

I sit by Kareem's side, watching him work. I feel a bit redundant. I have had tea made for myself so many times by kind Bedouin across the whole of St Katherine, and I am suddenly conscious that I have never done anything in return. Today, I decide to make an effort and when we have finished drinking, I take the glasses and wash them with bottled water, before placing them in the bag for Kareem. When we move on, I try to give wise ecological answers to the group's questions about the nature around us, but struggle to remember the species names of plants, birds, and bees that we see. When we stop for lunch, I am able to be more helpful, chopping the tomatoes and cucumbers for the salad, and clearing up the plates once we are done.

By late afternoon we make it to El-Kalm where we will spend the night. It is a smart Eco Lodge, with multiple stone buildings equipped with sustainable toilets and showers. We are welcomed by an old Bedouin man, who sits us all down and offers us tea. After we have rested and washed, we sit and eat by the warm fire, everyone telling stories and sharing tales about the trip so far.

When night falls, Kareem gets up and shows the guests to one of the big rooms. His plan is for them to sleep together, and for us to share our own private space. He comes back and sits next to me by the fire, and the old man squints at us with a frown.

"You two are not married," he says suspiciously.

"No, we are friends," I respond.

"You cannot sleep alone. You are not married," he says sternly, shaking his head.

"It will be all right. We are good friends and we have known each other for years," says Kareem, trying to argue for our privacy.

He fails. The man finds his own solution, placing all three of us in the other room.

We try to make the most of it. We place our mattresses at the far side of the room, with the old man sleeping next to the door. He sleeps noisily, rolling over often and snoring heavily. When I am sure he is asleep, I shift towards Kareem beneath our blankets and hold him close to me at last.

I am reminded of last springtime when we used to spend each night together. Our clothed bodies are touching once again, but we cannot connect further as the old man keeps guard all night. It is frustrating, and the following night there are no improvements. We spent the day walking back through the valley and have settled in a garden for the night. The tourists are camping outside beneath the stars, but Kareem and I will be sleeping in the hut.

I wish we had snuck out of the garden, the two of us walking together down the starlit valley with palms all around. Instead, we are in this hut, which is hot, stuffy, and small. Making things even less romantic is the presence of a young Bedouin guy who will also be sleeping in here, just one metre away.

I am pissed off. I thought I would get to spend time alone with Kareem on this trip, to lie together under the magnificent stars, but it is not going to happen. We are drifting apart. Perhaps, this is over.

## Chapter 33

I hear Mansour's motorcycle pulling into camp. I stay where I am, sitting alone in front of the camp's shop feeling miserable. Kareem had dropped me back at camp yesterday, still refusing to come in. The night in Wadi Itlah had not been fun, Kareem and I lying together beneath a blanket, just a metre away from our Bedouin friend. It was unsatisfactory. I do not know when I will see Kareem again. I tried to tempt him to visit my room in the dead of night, sneaking away before the sun rises, but he said no. He will not enter the camp.

Mansour comes and crouches down next to me. I smile and say hello, but he knows that something is wrong. I have hardly ever spoken to him about Kareem and me, our intimacies always staying in camp, but Mansour knows it all. He rolls up his cigarette and begins talking.

"Life is like a piece of string," he says wisely. "You have to measure it one hundred times before you make the cut. Cut in the wrong place, and it will be the wrong length forever."

He sounds like a prophet, who has worked out how this world works. I turn towards him and nod slowly. I cannot argue with his statement, but I do not know how it addresses my relationship woes.

He continues.

"Having a baby is the same as cutting the string. Once you have chosen it cannot be undone. Kareem cut his string in the wrong place."

Mansour is referring to Kareem's child. He pauses and looks wistful. He thinks about the length of his own string, the cut made by the boys he loves so much. They hold him here.

Once a baby is born, you are shackled by an unbreakable bond. You are entwined with another person, and in Kareem's case, to another place. When he moved to Slovenia nearly a decade ago, he thought it was fun and that he was free, able to return to the mountains whenever he chose. The birth of their daughter changed everything. He is now tied to the place, unable to forget about his child.

Mansour is right He is telling me how it is. Kareem has been drawn back here because of his homesickness, not knowing he would be torn in two, missing his daughter irreversibly. He does not have space in his life for others. He does not have room for me.

# *Chapter 34*

There is a small group of women gathering at the office, ready for a trip to the mountains. Kareem is their guide, and though he is still avoiding Fox Camp he is willing to meet them at the edge. I see him, and approach him from the terrace.

"How long will you be away for, Kareem?" I ask.

"Three nights," he replies, pushing his hand through his long, curly hair.

"We will not see each other again in that case. I am going to Dahab, to spend some time by the sea. So, this is good-bye," I say.

"Ma Salama Olivia, goodbye," he responds, stepping forward and firmly shaking me by the hand.

He says it with a smile, but I hold back my tears and cannot meet his eye.

I saw Kareem just once more during the rest of this week, the two of us spending an evening alone together up in Wadi Shraig. That was it. It hurts. Things have fallen apart between us.

Apart from that, I have hung out with Ben and passing tourists. I managed part of the Three Peaks Challenge with Ben and Leo, tolerating the presence of Abdul as the guide. I avoided looking in his direction and instead paid attention to the incredible scenic views. The route to Abas Bassa was long and tough, though, and by the time we reached its castle-lined summit the sun was close to setting and I was reaching my limit. I headed back alone, while the others went on to climb Mount Katherine and Mount Sinai in the dark night sky.

Ben has organised a big trek to climb the mountains this week. It is part of 'Sinai is Safe', a grassroots campaign that he has worked on with Bedouin leaders across South Sinai. It is at the height of the ISIS insurgency in North Sinai. By gathering men, women, and children from across Egypt to walk in these mountains, the so-called danger zone, Ben hopes that the perception of South Sinai as a dangerous place will change. This week he has a big group who will be staying at Fox Camp, where Rasheed and Suzy have agreed to host them in the tent before and after the climb. Ben sits with me telling me all about what is in store for his walking group.

Above us on the terrace, an old married couple sit drinking tea, angry expressions on their faces. They are retired Egyptian academics, both doctors, who have been coming here for years. They are furious at the new management who have ruined their experience and stripped them of their freedom in camp. They have both decided that they should never come here again. It disappoints me. Everything is changing.

That evening I sit in the tent while two tourists and their Bedouin guide are being charmed by Suzy. The Bedouin man recognises me, and we begin to chat. He asks me where my friends are and why it is so quiet. I tell him the truth, explaining that the camp now bans Bedouin from the tent, making them sit in the carpark, with no firewood or access to tea. He raises his eyebrows. Suzy glares at me, and smooths things over by offering the man another cup of tea. I get up and say my goodbyes. I cannot tolerate it in here. The atmosphere is so formal now. The magic is lost.

Despite the bad vibe, years of habituation draw me back to the tent, which remains the best place to sit and hide from the world. This afternoon, I am lying in the tent when I hear raised voices from outside, Ben and Rasheed shouting at one another. Rasheed has just told Ben that he no longer wants Ben's tourists in camp. The event is the day after tomorrow, and now the guests will have nowhere to stay. It is ruined. Rasheed has screwed Ben over.

Ben storms into the tent, swearing and shaking his head. He sits down on the cushions beside me and tells me what has happened. It is not fair. Rasheed appears at the tent entrance. He also looks furious. He rushes towards Ben, removing his sandal and trying to whack Ben with the shoe. I jump up and run out of the tent, looking back at the two of them who have started grappling. Everybody is standing around and watching the fight. Farag emerges in his large army jacket. He grabs the two men by their necks, pushing them away from one another and telling them off with a raised voice.

The group of people watching the show now move forward, driving Rasheed and Ben in separate directions. I move with Ben to the carpark tent, where other Bedouin arrive and sit with us to hear the news. I feel hurt and angered on Ben's behalf. I cannot understand why they refuse to accept business from him and, more importantly, how dare that man hit him.

Suzy steps in and begins to talk to Ben. She says that the incident never should have happened, acknowledging that her husband can be a bit extreme when he is angry. But she then tells Ben, "You should always, always treat Rasheed with respect."

She does not apologise. I stare at Suzy from the shadows. I cannot stand it; how dare she treat my friend like this? I cannot hold it in. I say quietly through gritted teeth, "Fuck you."

Suzy jumps to her feet in response to my whisper and screams, "Get the fuck out of my camp. Go and pack your bag right now. Get out!"

"Fine, I will leave immediately," I respond firmly, getting to my feet and marching straight out into the carpark, where I burst immediately into tears. I feel an arm around my shoulders, comforting me. It is Farag. He assures me that he will find somewhere for me to sleep, that there is likely to be a bed nearby and, if not, he will make space for me in his family home.

I go straight to my room and pack up my belongings. Farag then escorts me to the room at the base of Wadi Shraig. The building used to belong to my supervisor Francis and his wife Hilary. It is now empty, but beautiful. The bedroom has an en-suite and a tall, live tree forming the bedstead. I lie on the bed and try not to cry. I will get a taxi to Dahab first thing in the morning.

I love this place, but it is no longer my home.

# 2018

*Olivia in Fox Camp*

# Chapter 35

I have come back to Fox camp, but my life has changed dramatically in the meantime.

After Suzy kicked me out, I left first thing in the morning without saying goodbye or paying for my accommodation. Feeling guilty as I was driven away, I gave my taxi driver the cash to take back for Suzy. I spent the last few days of my trip alone in Dahab, where I told everyone I knew what Suzy had done to the camp. At night I had lain in bed and wept, chain-smoking packs of cigarettes and mourning both the loss of Kareem and the destruction of the place that I had once called home.

When I got back to England things moved on. Firstly, I passed my PhD, with no corrections. I have felt proud at many points along the way, like when my manuscripts about the benefits of the gardens on plants and pollinators were published in scientific journals, and when a previously unknown bee that I discovered was named after me, *Hylaeus oliviae*. But passing my PhD was very special and made me feel over the moon. My wonderful supervisors Francis and Markus were there to celebrate with bottles of fizz in the coffee room. I could not have done it without them. My friends brought me a beautiful picture of a bee which has pride of place in my house, and they got me terribly drunk in the pub. It was brilliant.

After that, things became more challenging.

I needed to get a job. My days were spent searching the web for postdoctoral research roles, finding so little, but applying to everything that was there. Eventually I spotted a six-month role on social media and snapped it up. The research project was exploring how the loss of tropical forest is affecting nature, people and climate in East Africa. It involved me moving to York, the most inspiring old city I have ever lived in. The cobbled streets, the leaning buildings, all overlooked by the Minster, a cathedral of magical proportions.

Before I started the new job in York, I had months of unemployment to fill. I was renting out my spare room in Nottingham and had enough savings to live off, but I had nothing at all to do. The solution was Romania. I got the chance to spend two months lecturing on a field trip in the Transylvanian farmland. We moved week by week between the rural villages, camping with the colleagues with whom I soon became friendly. My responsibility was to provide evening lectures for the students, but by day I often joined the other surveys. I avoided those that ran early morning or night, staying away from bird netting or small mammal trapping. Instead, I opted for the daytime strolls, monitoring the plants and the butterflies

The landscape was nothing like Sinai, but when I squinted it looked just like the rolling hills behind my family home in Bristol. When in focus, the hay meadows were packed with colourful wildflowers, brimming with crickets and incredible butterflies, and were so much more alive than the dandelion and buttercup fields of home. Nevertheless, when I lay amongst the flowers I felt transported back to my childhood, lying in the tall grass with our dog, Simba, a Rhodesian Ridgeback, with Meadow Browns fluttering around us. I missed that dog and still do. Reverie disturbed, I was brought back to the reality of the Transylvanian meadow by a charming but hungover student vomiting by my side.

In the midst of the Romanian hay meadows, Kareem decided to get in touch. One clear night I had walked behind a barn to find Wi-Fi signal on my phone and discovered had I received a photo from him. It was the full moon hovering above the mountains. I looked up at the same moon in the sky above me and felt an unavoidable reconnection with him and St Katherine.

After the Romanian trip, I went on to start the job in York, loving the city and the work I was doing, but even there, Kareem kept popping up. There were more photos of the moon, together with messages telling me how much he missed me, and one suggesting we got married. I know that he sent such silly and romantic messages to women across the globe, but they still made me miss him and want to return.

He also let me know that Suzy had been kicked out just months after I left. Farag Fox was back in control of his camp.

I had to go back, but the problem was that my professional life was getting in the way. After York I had interviews for jobs in Leeds, Cambridge, France, Germany, and New Zealand. All had been unsuccessful until now. I am a university lecturer! I could not believe it when I was offered the full-time job at Anglia Ruskin University in the centre of Cambridge. I have moved, buying a cute little terrace, and have made a new life for myself. Things have been so hectic, but I finally feel settled. I cannot drop everything and fly out for months like I used to, but I have booked some annual leave this Easter and will go back.

It was actually my mum who pushed for this trip. She brought it up while we were in an arty student café opposite the Tate Britain, where she mentioned her own desire to return to Sinai. Her sixtieth is coming up this June and she thinks those mountains are the perfect way to celebrate. I certainly agree. It is going to be a holiday, so we have had to find friends to join us. Everyone has heard me going on about the wonder of Sinai for years, but the problem is that the political situation has been scaring people off. The government has still rated St Katherine as 'Orange, Essential Travel Only', and the holiday industry has all but disappeared across Sinai, with no direct flights from the UK to Sharm El Sheikh. Despite this unnerving political drama, we easily recruited my old school friend Fran, who has visited me out there in the past. Although it was harder, we also managed to convince David, one of my university friends, and my mum's close friend, Kathleen, to join the party. It is an odd bunch, different ages and different backgrounds, but I am sure that the location is going to win everyone over. I am feeling excited!

## Chapter 36

The journey has been long. Because of the lack of direct flights, we had to fly via Istanbul en route to Sharm El Sheikh. When we arrived, the airport was quiet and virtually empty.

Outside, my lovely taxi driver Hameed was waiting for us, smiling when he saw me.

The subsequent drive was difficult. We got stopped by the police at the first check point, waiting several hours for enough tourists to join us in an armed convoy all the way to St Katherine. I got a horrible headache on the way, a migraine that made it hard for me to think. I curled into a ball and Fran tried to keep me entertained, filling the journey with a story, 'The Lion, The Witch and The Wardrobe' recalled from memory.

Now we are pulling into Fox Camp. I hope that we are all welcomed.

As soon as we enter camp I can tell that things are back to normal. Farag comes to greet us, giving me a warm embrace. Behind him there is Hamza, Jamal and Uncle Omar, all smiling and hugging me, shaking hands with my friends, and welcoming us all in. It is so good to be back.

We have arrived late, so after a cup of mint tea we head straight to bed. The next morning is relaxed and we lie in to rejuvenate ourselves. In the afternoon, I am ready to take everyone into the mountains. I am planning to lead us up Wadi Shraig and over into Wadi Arbien. We set off, following the path I have walked so often in the past. When we reach the garden, we stop to enjoy the view.

Kareem is there. He comes and says hello to us all. It is awkward. Fran and David know all about him and I have briefly mentioned him to my mum, but right now I am feeling embarrassed. When we set off again, Kareem calls out to me, warning me that we are not permitted to walk round into Wadi Arbien. The police have now set up a barrier at its base, preventing all from climbing through the valley. They want to stop Bedouin sneaking deep into the mountains where trouble and terror could arise.

The idea of barriers makes me furious. The police do not seem to understand the mountains. The pathways are all interconnected networks that make it is easy for the Bedouin, and me, to use alternative valleys and routes to reach the same point. Blocking Wadi Arbien alone is doing nothing other than restricting people's freedom, interfering with all of those garden owners that have homes there, and making me angry!

This is a holiday, so I try to bury my emotions and say nothing to my group. I lead us onwards, but instead of walking the circular route, we just turn around and come back down the way we came. It works out well, as when we pass Kareem's garden he calls us in and presents us with barbequed chicken and shish kebabs that he has cooked on the fire. He serves us a brilliant lunch, completely out of the blue. I do not know where the food came from or how he knew we were coming. As I sit by his side, I look at him and wonder why he is treating us like this. He is certainly impressing my mum and friends, but is he just trying to show off? Or is he really a kind and caring man who wants to make me happy?

Once we finish the tasty meal, we stroll back down to camp, the mountains orange in the glistening late afternoon sun. We drink tea and have a rest before dinner. Then it is on to the tent. Hamza is showing off, playing the drum and singing. My mum and Kathleen sip their tea and nod along smiling, but my mum feels conscious that the two of them are interfering with the party spirit. They are enjoying themselves but decide to head to bed early and rest for tomorrow. Once they have gone, the vibe changes. Fran, David and I unwinding as we clap louder along with the Sa'idi beat. I feel my shoulders relaxing, my body sinking back into the old life. I laugh at Hamza's nonsense and smile at dear Uncle Omar, who to my surprise has just given up smoking in a bid to become a healthier, older gentleman.

I stay up even later than my friends, keen to catch up properly with Hamza and learn what has been happening in his life. He has had another baby and his eldest boy has reached five years of age. The boy has started spending far more time in Hamza's life. He has actually lived here in Fox Camp, staying for months at a time, looked after solely by Hamza. I cannot believe Hamza has been acting so responsibly as a father. However, the thing that shocks me most is his new attitude towards women. He tells me about it in a slow and serious voice.

"Olivia, you know the women who visit the camp, I think that they do not all want me. I have learnt that some have husbands, boyfriends or that they just do not like me. They do not all want to have sex with me. So, I will stop," he says, looking at me intently. "I will stop trying now. I will not try to have sex with all the women," he affirms.

I burst out laughing and then congratulate him.

"Mabruk Hamza, well done. You have finally learnt that you should not try to have sex with all the women. Now you can just be kind to them and offer them tea. You have become a wise man," I say to him.

I have been telling him this for years. At last things are changing for the good.

# Chapter 37

In the morning, Mansour arrives in camp with a new, much smarter motorcycle. He greets me with a hug and smiles broadly at my mother, shaking her hand before I introduce him to my friends. He has been working extremely hard and has fitted us in between two other groups of tourists. We are heading up for one night in the mountains. We get going and it is great to be back walking with him; he fills me with complete trust.

My mum and Kathleen handle the mountains well, managing the climb despite the uneven path. Fran has been here before and is a confident climber, scrambling across the rocks and keeping right up at Mansour's heel, and David has slipped right into it. All of us are chatting and laughing as we climb, but progress is not as fast as it might be. The one thing that is slowing us down is my mum and Kathleen's unconstrained excitement about camels. I take the camels for granted these days but every time we pass one they squeal at one another, whipping out their cameras and stopping to get the holiday snaps.

The valleys are filled with wildflowers and walled gardens bursting with colour. I love being back. It soothes me. I hope that my friends are similarly won over by the place. We stop for lunch in a beautiful garden, where Mansour roasts aubergine beneath the coals, serving us baba ganoush with bread, cheese, and salad. After eating, he encourages us to sleep beneath the trees. I join him and immediately fall into a deep sleep. Everyone else enjoys lying in the cool shade and tries to doze, apart from Fran who prefers to roam, wandering distractedly around the garden.

After the break, we move on and by late afternoon we reach the long garden at the end of Wadi Zawateen where we are planning to camp. Mansour pulls out mattresses and blankets from the hut and we lay them out, ready to spend the night. We eat delicious chicken and rice, chatting and laughing as we go, my friends enjoying the night sky above us. I place my mattress near the fire alongside Mansour, with everyone else spread out along the garden. This all feels so normal to me, but my mum is feeling a bit apprehensive, not knowing where to go for a wee. There are no toilets, so she creeps outside the garden gate, walking through the dark until she finds a rock. She squats but struggles to pee, worried that everyone can hear her. When she gets back into her sleeping bag, tucked beneath the blanket, she feels her bladder still bulging and knows that she will have to sneak back outside once again before she can sleep.

The rest of us have managed to pee, feeling more relaxed about the mountain location However, sleep does not come easily because the full moon begins to rise. The bright white globe rolls over the valley top, illuminating all around us, casting the rocks in a silvery glaze. I stare at the moon for an hour or so before drifting off, but my mum still struggles to sleep. She wishes she had managed to empty her bladder in the darkness, now she will have to gain the courage to wee by the light of the moon.

I wake up to the sound of water boiling. I sit up groggily in my sleeping bag and Mansour hands me a sweet coffee. The others come and join us one by one as the sun warms them and they smell the breakfast cooking. Once we have all dressed and eaten, we start the second part of the journey. The plan is to walk back down Wadi Zawateen, but Mansour has planned an unfamiliar route leading us down into Wadi T'lah.

We stop in a garden that I am unacquainted with, situated high up on the valley edge. We all sit down on rugs outside a hut, joining an Egyptian lady who is there with her own guide. I have never seen an Egyptian woman travelling alone here. I have been aware of increasing numbers of Egyptian girls travelling in large student groups, but never on their own. I think the revolution is changing things, giving the women of Cairo more independence and the confidence to come here without male supervision. Earlier, in camp, we had bumped into a mother and daughter journeying together, the daughter taking wonderful photographs of Bedouin families. Now, up here we have met this lady travelling entirely alone. This never would have happened before.

As we drink tea, Kathleen begins chatting with the lady. Kathleen is amazingly sociable, making small talk easily in her charming Mancunian accent. She finds out that the Egyptian lady speaks immaculate English. She tells us that she studied at the University of Oxford, taking a Master's in Evidence-based Medicine. My mum's ears prick up as this field aligns closely with her work in Public Health. The lady continues telling Kathleen and my mum about her current project evaluating the proportion of Egyptian child births that are carried out by Caesarean section rather than naturally. It is much higher than other countries, perhaps because so many women find natural birth difficult and challenging because of their childhood genital mutilation. Though the C-section can help the delivery of the baby, for the woman the procedure is painful and takes time to heal. She concludes that it should only be done when there are problems with the birth, but worries that it is becoming standard practice for rich, Cairo mothers.

When we get ready to leave, the lady explains what has brought her here. She is extremely open, telling us that her work has made her stressed and anxious. She is here to visit Dr Khalid, a renowned herbalist who she hopes will give her medical advice, helping her recover and regain full health. I cannot believe that Dr Khalid is so famous. We will be visiting him in his garden tomorrow. I did not know that I was friends with a celebrity!

Mansour leads us onwards, over into a narrow valley that will take us down into Wadi T'lah. I remember coming here on the last day of my PhD trip with Sean, when Mansour had cooked a magical lunch and we slept in the spring sun. There are tall cliffs wrapping either side of the valley and no clear path, just boulders and scree to climb down. We reach a wide, flat slope and I stop. There is nothing to hold onto and the steepness makes my stomach spin. Everyone else has strolled down. I am sure I could do it last time, so I go slowly, my arms stretched out for balance, my legs wobbling, and my face screwed up with fear. At the bottom my mum is videoing me on her iPhone and everyone else is laughing. I am glad I am keeping my friends entertained.

I do make it down and we soon get back onto an established trail, making things easier for me. It leads us past a long monastery garden, with tall stone walls enclosing lines of olive trees. Once we reach the end, the taxi is waiting to take us back to camp. Instead of sitting for tea, we all head to our rooms, rushing to use the plumbed toilets and the hot showers to wash away the dirt. After dinner, we relax in the tent before heading for an early night. Getting an early night seems like a great idea but Kareem has messaged me and invited me to spend the night with him. I quietly leave my room and cross the olive grove, meeting him by the gate. Kareem takes my hand and leads me out into the wadi towards a garden along the base. We stop by the door and he searches amongst the rocks until he finds the hidden key and lets us in.

Kareem lays out a blanket beneath the apple tree and we lie down next to one another. We talk for hours about how our lives have changed. I have forgiven him for how he treated me last time I was here. We kiss and hold each other, gazing up at the swollen moon hanging above us, but nothing else. It is as if we are wrapping everything up. We have reached the end. We are saying our final goodbye.

## *Chapter 38*

I feel energised, even though I slept very little. I think I have been released, freed from Kareem and ready to enjoy the rest of our holiday. Our first activity today is to walk down to the monastery where I can show everybody the burning bush and the ancient artworks. We stroll down, first stopping at the 'Golden Calf', where cracks and crevices have created a calf in the pale yellow mountainside. We do not worship it like the idol it once was, but Kathleen enjoys taking photos for her album. When we arrive at the site of the monastery we stop at the shops, where Fran, David and I buy new Bedouin headscarves that will be perfect for protecting us from the sun. Next, my mum and Kathleen get drawn in by the young boys selling bits of rock, fossils, and crystals, sucked into buying these overpriced souvenirs that will doubtless look pretty on their bookshelves. I have never felt like a tourist before, always feeling that I live here and so have always politely declined the offers of tourist tat and handicrafts while I am drinking tea. Things are different this year; my mum and Kathleen are transforming me into a proper tourist and I will just have to enjoy it.

We move through the monastery, getting our tourists snaps, our sight of the gold-filled chapel, and Prophet Mohammed's handprint in the art gallery. Kathleen stocks up on religious books in the monastery shop and then we all stroll through the garden, past the long lines of olive trees, stretching out past the well-kept flower beds and stone terraces. This is the fourth time I have visited this place and it remains impressive, an unmatchable place to show your friends.

Of course, Dr Khalid's garden is equally special and that is where we are headed next.

Hameed is going to guide us through Wadi Itlah, since Mansour is booked up on another overnight trip. Mansour is getting so much business now, guiding new tourists who have been attracted by the professional Sinai Trail website. Hameed is completely different to Mansour, moving sleepily, with large, dark eyes and a face that looks undeniably stoned. I have known him for years, when he used to drive me to the start of the climb. He often invited me into his home for tea and food and I even received an invitation to his baby's naming ceremony.

Today, Hameed's wife serves us tea and nibbles before he drives us in his dilapidated car to the entrance of Wadi Itlah. We walk slowly into the wadi and along to the garden of Dr Khalid. It is a delight to see Dr Khalid again. I feel relieved that he remembers me without having Mansour, his brother, by my side. He smiles broadly as he greets me and shakes my hand before inviting us all into his garden for a tour. He walks us around, showing off the flowering herbs, the ancient carob tree, and the range of other fruit and nut trees.

Next, we are escorted into his hut, where we are made delicate herb-flavoured tea. He speaks very little English, and Hameed has little to say. Despite the lack of conversation with our hosts, we are all happy and relaxed. When we leave, the light is beginning to fade and it is evening by the time we return to camp. As we eat dinner, I see Ben running around anxiously. He has told me that he is hosting a group of rich Americans, who he hopes will invest in the extension of the Sinai Trail.

Ben's American guests have just got back from a two-day mountain trip and tonight he is hosting them in the tent, with music from the oud player and a visit from Sheikh Akeem. Ben needs the event to go well, he wants to win them over. We are invited to join the event, giving us all the chance to hear the beautiful music of the oud.

I have heard the oud player many times, with the same man invited to big events and parties. He is a charmer, always lifting his eyebrows seductively to the beat of his music, usually targeting his gaze at one person, Qasim. I always felt a little bit jealous.

We enter the tent and sit together, waving and saying hello to the American group sitting on the other side. One or two of them respond to us, but at the far end I can hear a man questioning what we are doing here, saying we are terribly dressed and looking like scruffs. It is offensive and I tense up, but I do not dare say anything out loud in case we are heard.

The music starts, but I continue listening to the chat of the American group. Apparently, they run a religious hiking trail elsewhere in the Middle East. They seem different to Ben. Ben loves the landscape. He has created deep relationships with the Bedouin, meeting Sheikhs from all of the tribes and forming impressive connections across the entire Peninsular.

In contrast, the Americans are extremely rich and focused on money. They are concerned about whether this is a serious, profitable business. They do not sound impressed by the mountains or the desert, rather they complain that the paths are not clear or signed, and there are no toilets. It is true that my mum, and now Kathleen, would really appreciate a portable toilet, but I have never heard the lack of facilities talked about with such venom.

Ben stands up in front of the group and announces that Sheikh Akeem will soon be joining us. The Americans may not be impressed by their Sinai trail so far, but they do sound very excited about the idea of meeting a Sheikh. The tent starts buzzing to the sound of the whole group whispering "Sheikh, Sheikh, oh man, Sheikh."

Sheikh Akeem walks in and begins shaking the hands of the awe-struck Americans. He is a tall, slim man, dressed in an immaculate white galabeya and a red head scarf. He is Qasim's brother and looks a lot like him, just older and much wiser.

I never knew him well, but two years ago I met him for coffee in London. Ben had worked wonders to get Sheikh Akeem a visa so that he could attend the astonishing ceremony where the Sinai Trail won the prestigious British Guild of Travel Writers Award. I was so proud of this much-deserved award, and it was also wonderful to meet up with Sheikh Akeem beneath the evening streetlights of London.

The Sheikh continues greeting the guests in the tent, each of whom stands up to shake his hand. When he reaches me, he knows exactly who I am, his face glowing with the recollection of our last meeting. He calls out my name, before embracing me with a warm hug, which I gladly return.

The group of Americans stare at me dumb struck. How on earth has this nobody of an English tourist managed to win the Sheikh's affection, when they have not. Life ain't fair.

# Chapter 39

This is our last day in camp. Time has flown by.

Today, we are heading down to the desert and then to the coast. Mansour has found the time to guide us and Qasim is driving, just like the old days. He pulls into camp in a new vehicle, a pick-up-truck with a long, open boot. It feels strange to see him after all this time and, as we hug, I notice that he has lost a lot of weight and looks tired. I hope his marriage is treating him well.

We say our goodbyes to everyone in camp, and then my mum, Kathleen, Fran, and David clamber into the open-aired back of the truck. Mansour jumps in after them, perhaps to keep them safe, and I sit in the front next to Qasim. We set off, getting past the first check point and out onto the open road. Qasim's first plan is to drive us out into the blue desert. It is a strange place, a piece of artwork where small mountains have been painted entirely blue. It has been skilfully painted by artists so that, from up above, you see the blue shape of a dove.

A bright blue dove. A sign of peace.

Qasim pulls off the main road and drives us towards the blue desert. We head across the bumpy rocks, everyone in the back holding on tight, until we meet another vehicle driving towards us. It is filled with armed police and, as we come to a halt, a serious looking plain-clothed detective walks towards us. Qasim gets out and begins speaking with the Egyptian detective. He is telling us to turn around, we are not allowed to continue driving through the desert. Qasim is not amused and begins negotiating with an increasing ferocity. He has driven across these deserts throughout his whole adult life, he knows every bump and turn, far more than this man who has come in from Cairo.

Mansour hops out of the back and tries to settle the argument, attempting to calm Qasim down. Qasim's voice is becoming raised, and he starts to shout at the armed police. I am beginning to feel nervous, particularly worried about the rest of my group who are sat in the open air without any protection.

All of a sudden, Qasim backs off, getting back into his truck and slamming the door. He turns the pick-up round and we head back the way we came. He lights a cigarette and says nothing, driving in an angry silence. I am with him. I have visited the deserts so many times and can't understand why the police are putting up these barriers. I feel hurt and frustrated that my past freedom to enjoy these landscapes has been destroyed and can barely grasp how angry Qasim must feel about them taking away the foundations of his life. As we continue driving, I see a young Bedouin boy hiding in the shack that we passed on the way out. He is crouched down, trying to disappear from trouble, perhaps from Qasim or from the armed police officers who are following behind us.

When we get back to the main road, we head back to Fox Camp, where Qasim offloads all that has happened to Farag. The rest of us drink tea and talk about the experience. It is then that Mansour makes things a little bit clearer. The problem was the pick-up truck. Apparently, they have made a law preventing tourists from travelling in the open boot, where they are exposed and at risk of terrorism or attack. If Qasim had driven us in his old Land Cruiser we would not have been stopped, and now would have been looking at the peaceful blue dove before gliding down the sand dunes.

After an hour or so we get back on the road, altering the plan so that we avoid the desert and dunes. Qasim remains cross as he has missed the opportunity to show my friends his driving skills and the wonders of the place. Instead of sand dunes, we stick to the road, coming to the starting point of our walk where Qasim simply drops us and says his goodbyes.

Now we are alone at the beginning of the White Desert, with tall rocks standing in front of an extreme drop into the valley. Mansour leads us straight towards the cliff edge. We have to descend a near vertical slope, with a frayed rope attached to help us climb down. Mansour goes first and we follow him one by one, while he waits beneath us to catch us if we fall. I feel terrified, but manage to make it down safely, feeling some company as I hear Kathleen squealing above me.

We move onwards, with the white rocks turning red all around us. Mansour stops in front of the second drop, this time to be navigated with the help of a metal ladder bolted to the stone. When it is my turn, I place my feet on the ladder steps and descend slowly, staring directly at the rock so that I cannot see the drop. I have no idea why Mansour has brought us on such a challenging climb. It is embarrassing; none of the others appear to be getting scared. It is me, the Sinai pro, who is finding things the hardest.

We reach the bottom and look up at the tall cliffs towering above us. This is the White Canyon. There are coloured horizontal stripes running along the cliffs, whites, oranges, reds, and browns, like a geological masterpiece. The path is narrow so we walk in single file, our feet indenting the pure white sand beneath us. Although this place looks devoid of life, there are hundreds of large, black beetles embedded in the sand. Some are slowly scrabbling around in the heat, but most of them are immobile corpses. Mansour explains that they have fallen from the top of the cliffs, not seeing the drop and unintentionally moving into this empty canyon that cannot support life. A tragedy.

The path begins to widen out, leading us downwards to a gulley of bright white rocks. This will lead us to Ain Hodra Oasis where we will be staying the night. I can remember climbing this route last time my mum was here. I have photos of Mansour waving a flag that he crafted out of a napkin, and others of me clambering down between the rocks.

I cannot do it today. I have just reached a drop, and beneath me everything is spinning, spiralling away. I am panicking. I cannot do this. I cannot.

Mansour sees that I have frozen. Without me speaking, he jumps back up the gulley and begins calming me. I do not know what is wrong with me, but Mansour does. He squats down right in front of the drop, so now all I can see is him and rock. He guides me down step by step and the vertigo melts away because all I can see is him. He talks to me gently as I go, until my breath calms, the rocks become flatter and the journey to the oasis feels achievable.

What a peerless friend.

# Chapter 40

The little boy is perched high on the back of the family camel, clinging onto the reins. His father was supposed to join him on foot but never came, so the boy and camel are all alone. His father was taking supplies to Ain Hodra and although the boy has been there a couple of times, he is not sure of the way. He looks around at the flat, rocky desert and does not know what to do. Nobody can see him and there is no point panicking, so he just keeps moving forward and hopes that the camel remembers the way.

Meanwhile, I calmed down as soon as we made it to the oasis. The sun is setting now as we had spent some time winding our way between the trees and gazing at the gardens from outside on the rocks, giving space to a teenage Bedouin girl up there chatting on her mobile. Now, the garden owner is cooking dinner and Mansour is lying on a rug looking exhausted. He has been guiding on overnight trips all week and could really do with going home to rest. He sighs. Tonight, we will be sleeping here, as we don't have a vehicle to drive us out into the cooler, mosquito-free desert. He just hopes that he will be able to sleep without any disturbance.

The sun is sinking, the sky a dark and dusky blue when a camel emerges from around the edge of the cliffs. As it comes closer, I see that a small, school-aged child is alone with the camel, no adults in sight. Mansour and the garden owner run over, helping the boy off and bringing him in to sit with us. He holds onto his knees and gazes at the strangers around him. His black eyes are wide and fearful, and he soon starts weeping silently.

Fran is brilliant, finding a ball and throwing it gently towards the boy. After a few tries he begins to smile, joining the game and throwing it back. We feed him and tuck him down beneath the blankets, hoping that he will be able to sleep. For the adults, my mum pulls out a bright yellow bottle and Mansour's tired face perks up. It is Limoncello, and reminds him of the last time we were here dancing with Beth in the light of the moon. The drink is poured out between us and we start to relax, looking up at the large bats swooping above us. Kathleen and my mum begin chattering with Mansour, having far more serious conversations than I have ever had.

He talks about his father and uncle who were pitted against each other during the Six Day War, one working with the Egyptians, the other with the Israelis. On one occasion, one of them had to hide from the approaching enemy, crouching behind a thorn bush before swimming across an entire ocean to get away. It was hard and dangerous work that both took seriously. But, despite being on opposite sides of the conflict, the two brothers would sit together and drink tea when they had the time. After all, they were family.

Mansour goes on to talk about a small mountain in the middle of the desert which has been entirely covered by rusting vehicles for decades.

"I do hope it wasn't Olivia's grandfather who put them there," my mum chips in with a laugh.

Mansour looks at her quizzically and she continues.

"After the Second World War he was based here in Sinai with the Royal Airforce Regiment. He tells a story of bringing his troops into the mountains and leading them all deep into a Wadi. He had misread the map. The valley narrowed and the vehicles got stuck between the rocks. Behind him was a long, long line of the three-tonne trucks he was in command of. I do hope they managed to reverse their way out!" she finishes, reducing us all to laughter.

I have also found out that both my mum and great-grandfather came here before me. My mum climbed Mount Sinai as a student, while she was staying in a kibbutz in the days when Sinai was part of Israel. In contrast, my great-grandfather came to Sinai with the Egyptian Expeditionary Force during the First World War. I had never heard about either of their tales when I started working here. Though I do not approve of the way the UK army interfered with life in these mountains, learning about my family history has made me feel more deeply connected to this place.

I feel a drop of rain on my forehead. Then another, and another. Before I know it, it is pouring down. I jump out of my sleeping bag and run towards the shelter. We had not noticed that the dark sky had been clouding up while we were drinking and laughing. Now we are all grabbing our sleeping bags and squeezing in beneath the rustic shelter, the poor little boy squealing with fear. Once everyone has lain down things do not get better for us. There are big, wet drips making their way through the dried palm-leaves that make up the roof, and there is no way that I can sleep.

Mansour is having the same problem. He jumps up and runs through the rain into the nearest hut. David and I follow him, the three of us spreading out our mattresses and sleeping bags in the dry hut. Mansour struggles to sleep. I can hear him sighing and rolling around, while David begins to breathe deeply. It is far too hot in here and I cannot bear to put my arms in the sleeping bag. Large buzzing mosquitoes are also sheltering from the rain and bite me at every opportunity. I hear Mansour move. He has had enough, so scoops up his mattress and returns outside to the damp shelter. I stay where I am for another hour, listening to the drumming of the rain, the buzzing of the mozzies and David snoring next to me. I cannot take it. I copy Mansour again and run back outside and hope for the best.

The night drags on slowly, wet and uncomfortable, and we are all pleased when we wake to a dry morning. We begin the day with tea and shakshuka, a dish of eggs, spices, and peppers. Here there are toilets and showers to keep my mum happy. The small boy looks keen to get home, grinning as we pack up our bags and Mansour loads up his camel. We set off on our way through the white, sandy desert, now with a clear blue sky above us. The desert is flat, but to our right is a tall, rocky cliff providing valuable shade. Although it is still early morning, Mansour pulls us over for tea.

The camel grazes happily as Mansour collects dried twigs for the fire. We all sit down in the shade, and I lean back on the rock and watch Mansour work. He still looks tired. The fire is now flickering, and Mansour starts rummaging in his rucksack. He pushes his arm deeper and deeper, and then realises that he left the kettle and cups behind in the oasis.

Mansour falls quiet. After a moment he begins removing the tea bags, sugar, and plastic cups.

"I may have forgotten the kettle and the cups, but I do have a solution," he tells us, holding up a clear plastic bag.

He starts filling it up with water when I call out.

"You cannot put plastic on the fire, it will melt!" I say. Mansour corrects me.

"No, not when it has water in it. The boiling point of water is lower than the melting point of this plastic, so with boiling water in the bag, it cannot melt," he says calmly and knowledgeably, tying a knot in the bag.

He then creates a wooden frame out of sticks from which he suspends the bulging bag above the fire.

After a few minutes the water begins to bubble without melting the plastic. Mansour is right. The boiling water has reached one hundred degrees which is not hot enough to melt the plastic bag. He does not look surprised.

Mansour picks up the coolest part of the bag, cuts it open and quickly pours the water into the cups which have been filled with tea. As he does so, the empty plastic bag crumples immediately into a tiny ball. It simply melts away.

As I sip my sweet tea, I marvel at the way it has been made. Mansour is an intelligent and creative man and if I had not known better, I would have believed that we had watched a miracle.

## Chapter 41

I take a big glug of water and tighten my headscarf around my head to keep off the sun. We have spent over two hours resting in the shade and the cool early morning has passed.

After drinking the plastic-created tea, I had gazed at the bright sun rolling up in the sky and had worried about the heat. I had considered suggesting to Mansour that we got going, making the most of the cooler part of the day, but did not dare question him. He did look worn out and was sat with his eyes closed, but he is a wise man and an unbeatable guide, so I said nothing.

Now it is extremely hot, though. We have passed all the shade-providing cliffs and now there is nothing but flatness. The rocky ground stretches out to the horizon, with clouds of white dust leading the way. The walk feels endless. I am walking with Fran, and together we are moaning child-like about the never-ending distance and the sun, laughing at our childishness as we go. Behind us, David is walking determinedly, but is beginning to feel dizzy. He is not wearing his headscarf, instead preferring the breeze through his hair.

The sun is beating down hard. We have been walking for hours and everyone has fallen silent, intent on just pushing forward. We are aiming for the road where a minibus should be waiting with our luggage, ready to take us to Dahab. Instead of being excited about the beach and the snorkelling that await us there, we are all tired and looking forward to crashing out on the journey.

I have run out of water and David's scalp has turned red, but the road is emerging in the distance. The camel has seen it and suddenly changes pace. With the boy on its back, the camel sprints away, getting smaller and smaller until they both fade away into the fuzzy horizon. Mansour says that the camel is taking the boy back to the nearby village. I really hope this is true, but all I can do is focus on walking.

I can see the minibus now and stare at the ground as we cover the final stretch. I sigh when we make it, sipping the ice-cold water brought by the minibus driver. Before we get going, we need to check that we have all our luggage, which has been brought to us from Fox Camp. The bags are lined up on the ground so that we can check that ours is there.

David's is not there. He is not happy. His bag contained his expensive headphones and he is convinced someone must have stolen it. He begins stomping back and forth, fuming about the theft. I try to placate him. I do not believe that people in camp would steal from my friend.

There must have been a mix-up. His bag was probably just left behind, an accident rather than a theft. Mansour rings the camp and tries to arrange a redelivery to David in Dahab. There is nothing else that can be done by the side of the road, so it is time to say goodbye. I give Mansour a big hug, as do the others. Then we pile into the minibus and get going.

The minibus has air-conditioning, which lightens the mood. We start chatting and laughing again, apart from David who remains hot and cross. Kathleen's phone buzzes and she reads that her daughter has just got a place at medical school. Kathleen is delighted and proud. Her happiness is infectious. It spreads to us and begins preparing us for the last stage of our holiday.

When we arrive in Dahab, I feel relieved and am ready to rest. We all eat out, enjoying the restaurant food and a refreshing beer by the sea, but the long desert hike has made us ready to sleep. David still does not have his luggage, so has nothing except his dusty desert bag. Despite this, he still collapses under the bedroom fan in the clean white sheets, sleeping deeply until morning.

## Chapter 42

David's bag is safely delivered in the morning, reuniting him with clean clothes and his valuable headphones. I tease him over breakfast.

"See, David, I told you that the Fox Camp staff can be trusted. They are my friends, so they respect you," I say, smiling.

"Oh, alright. I should have trusted you," replies David.

He is relieved to have his bag back. It cheers him up, and together we all become excited about the ensuing two-day holiday by the sea.

After breakfast, I sit drinking another milky coffee, while the others pack their bags for the day. Opposite me is a handsome, smartly dressed Englishman, who turns around and smiles.

"Good morning. How are you enjoying this lovely place?" he asks.

"Oh I love it!" I reply.

We begin chatting and he tells me about his career.

"I am based at the Embassy up in Cairo. Ah, this is a wonderful country. Do you know anything about the Egyptian culture?" he asks.

"Well, I know quite a bit. I have made friends with lots of the Bedouin, working up in St Katherine for years now. I know a lot less about Cairo though. How long have you been here?" I reply.

The man shifts in his seat, surprised to discover that I am not just a transient tourist. He hides his embarrassment professionally and explains to me that he has been here for six months so is very familiar with the city. He also tells me about his Egyptian girlfriend. She is amazing. She is upstairs in their bedroom, probably sorting her makeup and hair for their day out. She has been up there for at least two hours and he is feeling a little bit restless, so he decides to go up and check on her. He stands up, shakes my hand, and says goodbye.

At that point, Fran and David appear, followed by my mum and Kathleen. I jump up, slip on my flip-flops, and off we go, strolling together down the seafront, exploring, and browsing in the shops. Everything is clean and bright, recently painted and done up. It is Easter, and the street is filled with Egyptian tourists enjoying the break. There are whole families and couples holding each other's arms and smiling at one another. Lots of the women are dressed in brightly coloured headscarves, while many others are wearing pretty dresses with their long hair flowing loose.

When I first came here, the hotels and restaurants were filled with Russian, German and English tourists, most of them here for the diving. In the following years, the flights stopped and the world appeared gripped with fear due to the revolution. Dahab became empty, with few tourists other than travellers and expats. Things crashed. Hotels and restaurants went bust and closed down and everywhere else looked tired, paint peeling and seats empty. It is wonderful to see things alive again. We walk past the thriving shops, the dive centres and all the restaurants, and many of the staff recognise me even after all these years.

I take us all down to Yalla Yalla bar where we can lie on the cushioned seats, enjoy the sun or the cool shade, and swim in the clear sea. Everyone but me heads off to hire snorkels and flippers, before climbing down the stone steps to see what is down there, leaving me to enjoy a sheesha pipe in the shade.

I am the only one who does not like snorkelling. Knowing that I will stay behind, I have nonetheless recommended that they take their snorkels and visit the Blue Lagoon tomorrow. It is an incredible place, brilliantly beautiful from both above and below. The lagoon has corals all around the edge, with the circular centre a pale but intense blue. The dark, deep ocean surrounds the lagoon, where the colourful life of the coral reef simply vanishes. The lagoon is extremely deep, and at one point in the coral is a human-sized hole that leads out into the sea. Divers are attracted to this, like climbers are drawn to Everest, but over one hundred have died while trying to swim through.

The lagoon is safe for snorkellers, though. When I went there, I swam slowly around the coral edge and looked at the astonishing rainbow of marine life. There were fish of all shapes, sizes, colours, and patterns, weaving their way through the forest of corals. I should have loved it, but the problem was that there was no air. I am terrible at snorkelling, and I felt squashed, claustrophobic and unable to breathe. There were also the jelly fish.

In the morning I wave them all off, taking it easy and getting ready for a proper relax. They ride the bumpy taxi trip to get to the lagoon while I lie in the morning sun before wandering down to my favourite spot. On my walk, I notice the gentleman who works in the Embassy. He is walking with his partner, who is dressed in a silky mini-dress, her long, black hair waving down her back. She looks fabulous, but he is unable to hold her arm, as he is bent over and pulling their three enormous suitcases.

I spend the rest of my day enjoying my favourite calamari sandwich, drinking beer, and smoking apple sheesha in the sunshine. When I get too hot, I climb slowly down the steps into the cool sea and swim out, gazing back at the multi-coloured restaurants that wrap around the bay. I lie on my back, floating and thinking of Beth. Every time we were here we sang a line inspired by a song from the film 'Bedknobs and Broomsticks', which Beth taught me, and I will never forget.

"Bobbing along, singing this song, at the bottom of the beautiful, briny sea," I sing. "Have a BANANA!" I finish, lowering my voice theatrically. I hope that nobody is listening.

Those were the days. It is not quite the same without Beth.

The others loved the Blue Hole, seeing an incredible array of fish, while I made the most out of Yalla bar and kept my head above the water. After we are all washed and dressed, we go out for our last supper. We choose the poshest looking seafront restaurant, which is dimly lit and filled with deep cushioned seats and draped with delicate Arabic fabrics. The waiters are smartly dressed and serve us platters of dips and home-made bread, followed by mains of fresh seafood. This is nothing like dinner in the desert, but it is a perfect way to end our holiday.

Together we walk back past the bright restaurant lights that glimmer on the sea front. Back at Bedouin Lodge, our hotel, we sprawl contentedly on the cushions and order cold beers to end our evening. Ahmed brings the drinks over as Kathleen whips out a brand-new pack of cards.

"Let's play," she says, full of enthusiasm.

We decide to play *Bullshit*, taking it in turns to discard cards face down in the centre of the table.

"The cards look fuzzy. I can hardly read the numbers," I say quietly.

"Ooh, is it an excuse not to win," says David fondly.

"No, I am serious," I respond.

I can see the colours, red versus black, and the suits, but they are out of focus.

"It is quite dark in here," says Fran.

"Or maybe it's because of the hot sun," says Kathleen.

I am not sure about these explanations. I shrug and return my cards, preferring to lie back against the low cushions and listen to them play. It has been so good to come back to this place, to see my friends in Fox Camp, to walk in the mountains and swim in the sea. People here cannot even get visas for the UK, but I can fly back and forth whenever I want. It is such a privilege.

I close my eyes and let out a contented sigh. I love this place. What a lucky life.

# NEW WORLD

*The proton therapy mask*

# 2018

*With brother, Tim, at his wedding*

# *Chapter 43*

Beep, beep, beep, beep.

The bleeping is continuous, and everything smells sanitised. I hear my name being called as I wake, the voice becoming louder and clearer. It is the neurosurgeon. He holds his identification card up to my face and asks whether I can read his name. His face is blurry. I concentrate and I can read the letters on his card one by one. He tells me, "Well done" so I close my eyes, falling back into a deep sleep, blocking out the sounds of the ward.

I have been diagnosed with a brain tumour. It is a large meningioma, a benign brain tumour that is pressing on my optic nerve and the cranial nerves surrounding it. I have just had surgery to try to retain the sight in my left eye and prevent me from going completely blind.

I rarely mention it, but I am blind in my right eye. It is an artificial eye, a "glass eye", which I have had since I was a baby. In my baby photos, the flash turns my healthy eye red, while the other looks white, and my medical parents recognised it as a rare eye cancer called retinoblastoma. I had my right eye removed at the age of six months, but the cancer came back. They thought I would die, but a combination of chemotherapy and radiotherapy saved me. It was pioneering treatment then, rarely used on eyes and faces, and it worked, but nobody ever told me that it would put me at risk of growing a meningioma later in life.

I am so used to my artificial eye that I do not think to tell people unless they ask. When I was child things were different. I often took it out in the school playground, kids laughing at the strange eyeball and intrigued by my empty, pink eye socket. I stopped seeking attention when I grew older and, as a teenager, I was upset every time someone peered at my face. Children would not hide their fascination and often stared, some smiling, others frowning. I hated it. It often pushed me to tears.

I am misshapen, the childhood radiotherapy having slowed the growth of the right side of my face. I wanted to look normal. I remember staring at my face for hours during an art lesson, having to sketch a portrait of my wonky face. I could not forget it, and by the sixth form I had become depressed, on one occasion smashing my bedroom mirror on the floor so that I didn't have to look at my reflection.

My parents have taken care of me at every step of the way. When I was eighteen, they got me an appointment with a maxillo-facial team in Birmingham, who proposed facial reconstruction of the right side of my face to create balance. It was what I wanted, but the treatment would take months, requiring me to spend days at a time sitting in a hyperbaric oxygen chamber down in Devon before the surgery could even start. I would have to give up my entire summer. I could not handle that, so I decided that my face was okay.

Instead, I was able to complete a Fine Art foundation degree, and then spent the summer travelling in Namibia and South Africa. I volunteered with 'Elephant-Human Relations Aid', a charity that helps build peaceful relations between desert elephants and local communities. My group was responsible for building walls around water pumps in the middle of the Namibian desert to keep the elephants out.

During this trip I met James, a beautifully handsome man, both intelligent and funny. I have wonderful memories of us sitting together, watching the astonishing elephants playing in an isolated lake, and of the two of us lying together by the fire surrounded by the enormous sky. I was awoken to the magic of life and stopped caring about what I looked like.

It is great not to care too much about your appearance, but please pay attention to symptoms, and to change. I think my face has been swelling for years and I have ignored it. I have had the headaches, the migraines, the tingling down the left of my face, the dizziness, the slowing down, but I denied it all. My tumour is at least six centimetres in every direction, around the size of a satsuma. It is big. It explains it all.

Perhaps I knew about the tumour. I had run internet searches for symptoms like headaches, migraines and neuralgia, and brain tumour was always there at the bottom of the page. I felt sick about it. I once tried to raise it with my parents in a London bar where we were having a nightcap after a celebratory evening out in the West End, but it did not register. I didn't know about the risk of developing tumours from the type of radiotherapy I had had as a baby. It had been new and under development; it is much safer now.

# *Chapter* 44

My tumour was diagnosed in the week I got back from Sinai. During the week after the card game my vision kept getting worse. I presumed, or pretended, that it was caused by my migraine. I kept working and had plenty to do in the evenings. First, I saw Beth and we attended an excellent talk about improving the sustainability of our planet. I was able to see Sir David Attenborough giving the closing remarks, but Beth kept frowning at my peculiar behaviour. My eye would no longer look to the left, so every time I wanted to look at her, I had to turn my entire head. She was worried but kept it to herself.

I went on to see friends for drinks by the river, and then joined my colleague, Helen, for a talk by Simon Amstell. His words were funny and inspired, but I could not even see his face. Helen made me promise to ring 111 in the morning. I did as I said, and the 111 staff insisted that I head straight to the local Accident & Emergency Department in Cambridge. I could not see well enough to walk to the hospital, so I got a taxi. The taxi driver was irritated when I could not find my cash to pay him, but he did direct me to the A&E entrance.

I waited for hours. When I eventually got to describe my symptoms, I attributed them to a bad migraine and so was not taken too seriously. It was late evening by the time that I was thoroughly examined. The doctor was puzzled by the fact that my eye did not turn to the left. She asked me how long this had been the case, and then asked to look at the photographs on my phone that showed the worrying and gradual occurrence of the symptom. If I had two eyes, I would have noticed this much earlier because it would have caused troublesome double vision.

The consultant then popped in and suggested that I went home and waited for my migraine to fade. I burst into tears. I live alone, and right now I cannot see enough to cope. I need help. This made them decide to send me for some scans. After the head scans, I sat alone in the dark and empty eye clinic, feeling scared and confused. It was gone ten o'clock when I was collected by the female doctor who told me softly that the scan had revealed a tumour and that I needed to spend the night on the ward. I did not know what to do or think, so I simply told her that I was hungry because I had not been able to eat anything that day. The wards had stopped serving food, so she bought me a panini as she guided me through the labyrinthine hospital corridors.

I started crying when we reached the ward. The kind doctor offered to ring my parents and tell them what has happened. My mum and dad set off at four in the morning on their three-hour drive from Bristol to Cambridge. Before leaving, they rang my Aunty Ali who lives nearby, and she was with me in an hour. I could hardly speak to her but crumpled into her arms and covered her in tears. I was supposed to spend the night in the hospital bed, but Ali got us into the guest room where we could cry in private. I lay down on her lap, wrapped in a blanket, shaking with shock and fear.

"Oh my darling Livvy," she said as she stroked my hair. "I know that you are going to be alright. I prayed to God while I was driving here asking for you to stay alive and strong. I know my prayers have been answered because the traffic lights stayed green the whole time. It was a sign. The lights were bright green, my darling girl, and I sped through them knowing that you are going to survive."

I do not believe in Gods or prayer, but it helped having her there.

My memories of the ensuing days are foggy.

My parents arrived in the morning. They were both devastated. I had never seen them that upset in my life. My brother arrived the following day, which meant that were all present for the discussions with my neurosurgeon. The first step, he explained, was to take a biopsy from the tumour to establish whether it was benign or malignant. Although he suspected it was benign, any decisions about surgery could not be taken without a clear tissue diagnosis.

The tumour has grown through the base of my skull and is invading the space at the back of my nasal airways. I am told that this is easiest place to biopsy the tumour so a few days later an ENT surgeon undertakes an examination under anaesthesia and a sample of tissue is sent for histology. Results confirm that I do have a low-grade, benign meningioma.

With the diagnosis confirmed, further discussions with my neurosurgeon take place to plan surgery. My tumour is large. It is compressing my left optic nerve and encasing other cranial nerves and vital structures. It will be impossible to remove the tumour in its entirety, he tells us, and so more limited surgery is planned to try to debulk the tumour from around my optic nerve in the hope that this will save my sight.

My parents and brother are all worried that this tumour will kill me, but I have such different views and feelings to the rest of my family. I feel that the discovery of the tumour provides a solution. My sight has been deteriorating, but now I know why and the proposed surgery should make things better.

I returned home before the surgery feeling strangely numb. I spent the following five days soaking up the spring sunshine. My friend, Fran, visited and we lay in my local pub garden, where I naughtily smoked and drank a pint. I was on sick leave, but my students saw me in the pub on several occasions, completely unaware of the reality of my situation.

My brother told me that he loved me so much that he needed me to survive. With a laugh he said that it did not matter if I lost sight or went blind, the important thing was to live. He slept by my side on the night before the surgery. It is something we never do, and I felt like we were children again. I did not sleep well.

Early the following morning I was in hospital ready for surgery, feeling terrified about losing my sight.

I had been prescribed oral steroids to reduce the swelling around the tumour in the hope that this would relieve some of the pressure on my optic nerve. A week of taking these drugs had restored my sight and now I looked around with my temporarily perfect vision and saw the consultant and anaesthetist looming above me. They looked ominous but spoke to me kindly, asking me to count down from ten. I did as I was asked, and I faded out of consciousness, leaving behind the world I had known.

My family were not sure how to fill the time of my surgery. Instead of waiting in the hospital for the several hours involved, they decided to make the most of the sunshine and so headed out for a pub lunch. While they wait nervously, the surgeon cracks open my skull and scrapes tumour away from my optic nerve.

Post-operatively I feel drained. I am trapped in a hospital bed, with blurred vision, puffy eyelids and an enormous swollen cheek that is stopping me moving my mouth. I start to cry. At first the tears drip silently from my eyes, but now I am sobbing loudly, my whole body is shaking. None of the doctors or nurses come to console me. I see the blurred outline of a woman coming towards me, but she says nothing, instead pulling the curtains around my bed and hiding me from the ward. I know I should be happy that I have survived my brain surgery, but I have lost my sight. I am distraught. My cheeks are painful and swollen, my eyelids will not open, and I cannot make out the faces around me. How can I do anything but cry now that I cannot see?

I weep continuously about the loss of my vision. Perhaps the staff don't understand, certainly none of them try to comfort me. Instead, I am referred to a psychiatrist who visits me in my hospital bed and asks me a formal list of questions. It is clear to me that his main focus is on whether I am likely to commit suicide. I love my life, why would I want to die? The psychiatrist soon realises that I am just understandably devastated because I have lost my sight.

## Chapter 45

I am staying in Bristol with my parents while I recuperate.

Now that I have been discharged, my main emotions are pain and suffering. During the operation they shaved the front of my scalp so that they could crack out a square of my skull for access. The bony plate that was removed has been pinned back into place but will take time to heal. This creates stress enough, but the surgery has also created a range of complications. There is a lot of swelling stretching down the left of my face, putting increased pressure on a range of nerves. I have felt tingling in my cheek for some time, but now it is far more painful and intense, as if I am getting repeatedly electrocuted. My forehead is frozen, unable to move. My eye still cannot turn to the left, my tears have stopped working and I cannot focus on text or images. It is difficult.

My vision has always been poor. I wear contact lenses throughout the whole waking day, because without them I am extremely short-sighted, $-8.75$ dioptres. I cannot wear lenses now as my eye is dry and swollen. My glasses were smashed just before surgery, but I don't think they would even work at the moment. My eye can now open a little, but all I can see are vague colours and shapes. Everything and everyone appears blurred and out of focus, and I cannot see things up close.

There has been a lot of damage and I just hope that it will heal.

My parents are doing everything they can to help me. Coffees are provided, meals are cooked, and hugs and kindness are there on demand. It is extremely difficult for them. They do not have the physical pain, but they must watch it in me, their daughter and cannot do anything to make it stop. During the day, my mum must go into the university where she works but Dad has just retired from the local medical practice. He is on a mission to keep me occupied and distracted. He is sure that moping on the sofa and sneaking behind the shed for a cigarette is not enough to heal me. I need to get out of the house.

My first trip out is to the seaside at Weston-super-Mare. Dad is going to get his car serviced and has insisted that I join him. I did try to say no, but he has won. There is nothing to do at home; I cannot see my phone, computer or the TV, so I cannot think of an excuse. I stay silent in the car, worrying about what will happen. When we drop off the car, I cling onto Dad's arm as he leads me through the busy streets towards the coast. We walk along the promenade. I can make out the brown sand and white breakers of the sea stretching out beside us. There is a strong smell of the salty sea, a cold wind on my shaved head, and everything looks grey and fuzzy.

We approach the arcade at the end of the pier and are greeted by loud bleeps and painfully bright flashing lights. I refuse to go inside, but Dad has spotted a huge deck chair provided for comical photo opportunities. He insists that I get into it as he wants a snap to share with the family. I scramble into the huge chair, holding back a smile when he takes the shot.

We leave the pier and continue along the promenade. On reaching the end of the walk we turn back and start retracing our steps. I remain quiet and sullen but Dad is persistent, determined to cheer me up, so the next stop is the Crazy Golf course.

"Well, I won't be able to do it. This is a stupid idea," I complain as he buys the tickets and hands me my golf club.

Undeterred, he leads us onto hole number one and places my ball down. I cannot distinguish the edges of the sphere, but its bright red colour stands out against the green artificial turf. I go for it and whack the ball, moving it closer to the hole. I get the hang of it and hit it time after time, making it pass the obstacles and into the holes. I get a hole in one, but more importantly, I am beating my dad and am beginning to laugh and smile. I did not think I had the vision to do this, but the blurry shapes are good enough to let me win. Our last stop is for lunch. We sit at an outdoor table overlooking the sea. Dad buys me a pint and we make a toast to good health. The first cool sip of beer releases something in me, reminding me how good life can be.

Over the coming weeks the sun arrives and the flowers bloom. It is a spring of healing. My dad and I start walking through the local Mendips hills, fields of bright green and skies of blue. We discover a new wood and fields covered in the blurry, purple-blue of wild bluebells. At weekends we walk with Mum by the river, and when my brother visits, we climb to get a view of Chew Valley Lake. The shapes and textures of the plants and flowers remain hidden, but the bright colours of the landscape sparkle in front of me. We have been on walks like this in the past, but now I am feeling lucky to be alive and gain an added sense of joy in this beautiful landscape of my family home.

In June it is time to return to Cambridge, back to my independent life. But first I have a wedding to attend. An old school friend who I have known since I was eleven and remained best friends with throughout our school years is getting married in Edinburgh, and I am going to stay with my brother in Newcastle on the way. My parents drop me at Temple Meads, Bristol's busy railway station and I make my way through the crowds. I get through the barriers using an e-ticket on my phone and manage to make it down to the underground corridor that leads to the platforms. The platform numbers are in numerical order and brightly lit, making them stand out and easier to navigate. However, the centres of the numbers are blurred. I have started wearing my glasses now but have lost the periphery of my vision so need to shift my head from side to side to work out the platform numbers. I succeed, making it onto the correct platform and then onto the Newcastle train.

Tim picks me up at the other end, navigating us through the enormous and unfamiliar Newcastle station. It is great to see him and his fiancé Steph, and we spend the evening relaxing happily together and snuggling up with Norman. Well, I want to snuggle up with Norman. He is a fox terrier, their handsome little dog. He is adored by all but is not interested in affection, and instead spends the whole night dropping his toy at my feet and insisting on never-ending games of tug-of-war. He really is not keen on a hug.

The following day, Tim and Steph are both working at the local hospital, so it is just me and Norman. I feel that it is my duty to take the little chap for a walk, so set out to the local park that is just a few streets away. We get there easily, and Norman runs around happily on the extendable lead. Problems arise on the way back. I think logically and manage to get us to a street corner, but I cannot read the street sign. I peer closely and move my head around, but it does not help. Doubting my sense of direction, I turn around and go back the way I came. Suddenly, I feel dizzy and confused. I panic and let out a whimpering cry. It is then that Norman reacts. He starts pulling on his lead, back to the previous turning and then uses all his energy to drag me down the street and into their front doorway. Either he knew that I needed his help or, maybe, he was just a dog who really wanted to get home, but I love him for it. I head straight for the sofa, where he joins me and licks me as I cry. He curls up close to me and I twist my fingers through his fur as his thick coat absorbs my tears.

# Chapter 46

I close my front door and feel Zambia winding herself around my legs. After visiting my brother in Newcastle, I attended my friend's wedding in a sunlit grove of the Edinburgh Botanic Gardens. It was a beautiful occasion. I got to catch up with the bride and her family and had fun being pulled around the dance floor in a Ceilidh, but now it feels brilliant to be back home

"Yo bro! Welcome back!" calls Lilly as she runs down the stairs.

Lilly is my housemate. She is younger than me and is pursuing her dream of becoming a news reporter. Her current job is covering local news stories from across Cambridgeshire that her employer then sells to the national press. This involves interviewing businesspeople and members of the public, sometimes having to knock on victims' doors to get a story or, on other occasions, spending hours sitting in court reporting criminal cases. It is hard and emotionally draining work, and she is paid very little. It is a big shift from her last job, which had a much higher salary. She was a pole-dancer in Australia, semi-naked, but never going further, just earning herself a bomb of cash.

Lilly sits down on the stairs and starts chatting about what has happened while I have been away. She is slim, with brown skin and long black hair, wearing her favourite bright pink jacket, and is peering at me through the banisters. We have not known each other long, but can talk for hours, discussing news, science and how to save the world. Zambia is her cat, who she brought here as a kitten when she moved in nearly a year ago.

Zambia is a tiny cat, with soft black and brown fur. She is well behaved, but reluctant with affection. She is half the size of the fluffy Katkoot of Fox Camp and, despite the differences, I am beginning to adore her. Lilly keeps her bedroom door firmly shut at night and my affection is only reciprocated at about three in the morning when Zambia sneaks into my room and wakes me. She jumps on my bed, rubs my face, and then lies down beside me for an hour of cuddles. It is worth waking up for.

When I was called into hospital for the biopsy of my tumour, I was put in a bed opposite a woman who was extremely keen on cats. She found out about Zambia and then talked endlessly about how I must miss her, how it must be making me so sad. Although I am really fond of the little cat, on that day I was more preoccupied with my diagnosis with a major brain tumour. I hope Zambia still loves me and does not hold this against me.

Now I am back home, my primary goal is to return to work. I have spoken with my manager, and the plan is to acquire a large computer screen. I will place it at the edge of my desk, increase the font size, use a screen magnifier and hold my nose right up to the screen. It should be fine. It is also the summer holiday so I can use the time to prepare lectures and practice before the students come back.

But before I return to work there is another wedding to attend. This one is my brother's. He and his fiancée have decided to get married in a chateau in the Aquitaine region of the South of France, where they once went on a romantic holiday. I am extremely excited about my little brother getting married, although I had hardly registered that he was grown-up enough for such a thing. My new dress is packed along with summery clothes for our pre-wedding holiday, and I head off on my own to Stansted airport for my flight to Bordeaux. I make it there on the train, and then navigate check-in and boarding without major difficulty. When I get on the plane, I experience the first real challenge. I cannot read the seat numbers, seeing nothing but blurs. I ask the person in front of me to show me to my seat and she does so happily. I do not have a white stick or anything else to indicate my visual impairment, so people are not aware of my post-surgery sight. It feels embarrassing.

Mum, Dad and Grandma are waiting for me when I arrive in France. We are spending the week together in 'Lortal', a big gite with a bright green garden and an enticing, turquoise swimming pool. It is great to spend the time with my Grandma Louise, my maternal grandmother. She is a small, pale woman, who is wise and kind. She is always there for me. On our first day, we are both in the kitchen when I need to rant. I cannot make coffee. It is not safe for me to pour boiling water from the unfamiliar kettle into the unfamiliar mugs, and it is so difficult for me to see my way down the dark, wooden staircase. Grandma listens patiently to my outburst, and then gently recommends that I find the solutions. I can ask my family to make me hot drinks, they are here for me, and yes, the stairs are hard, but I am able to get outside and enjoy the sun.

I take Grandma's advice and start to relax. Days are spent lounging by the pool and swimming increasing lengths with Mum. We start with twenty-five lengths, increasing to fifty, and then one kilometre and ultimately one mile. We swim slowly, talking as we go, while Grandma watches us from the shade, her book on her lap. Grandma has not swum for five years and we are determined to get her into the cool, blue waters. We eventually succeed, and by the end of the week she joins us, floating on the brightly coloured noodles and laughing in the sunshine.

The week flies by, with my dad out cycling while we enjoy the pool. Mum takes photographs of the butterflies that cover the lavender bushes and as the sun sets, we stroll along past the golden orchards and the deep green olive trees. We feast on fresh baguettes and delicious French cheeses. One day we visit a vineyard at Chateau Tiregand with Tim, Steph and her family, where we have a tour and then taste the fresh white wines and deep reds available for sale, picking the best to be served at the wedding.

We move to Chateau La Thuiliere the night before the wedding. My parents are placed in an enormous double room, with a beautiful balcony and bright orange tassels hanging in a doorway that leads into a grand bath and shower. I am staying with Grandma in a room opposite, which is small, plain, shaded and altogether more modest. It is good enough for us, but right now I am lounging on my parent's huge bed as we prepare for tonight's pre-wedding party. We all head out to the beautiful garden, where tables are laid for the thirty guests. During the afternoon, Tim's old school friends have been dive-bombing in the Chateau's swimming pool, but now everyone is dressed smartly and are ready to be served. The pre-wedding night is wonderful, a chance to chat with Steph's family and to meet the friends. The food is delicious, and we drink more than we should. As I fall asleep beside Grandma, I cannot wait for the wedding itself.

Today is the day. I dress up in my new dress and my mum helps me put on makeup and curl my hair, disguising the shaved side of my head which has nearly grown back. The service is being held outside and is scheduled for four in the afternoon, when they hope it will be cooler. It is not; the sky is still deep blue, and the sun is intense, making my brother and his best man sweat beneath their tuxedos. My brother is pacing around, checking on the flowers and chairs that are beautifully aligned and ready to go. We all sit down, and the music begins. The bridesmaids head down the aisle in their beautiful pale purple dresses, followed by Steph, the bride. I cannot see people's faces, but I know that Steph is glowing. Her long, brown hair is shining, her skin is tanned, and her glistening white dress flows around her. The service is led by a humanist celebrant. As it begins, I hear my brother laugh. I cannot make out what is going on and feel a momentary sense of panic. All is okay though, and the service proceeds smoothly. The bride and groom say their vows, exchange their rings and declare their love for each other.

They are husband and wife. It is time to celebrate. First we have champagne and fancy canapes, accompanied by live guitar music in the background. Then there is dinner, wine from the Chateau Tiregand vineyard and speeches from Tim, the best man and Steph's dad. Then it is time to dance. The musician switches from his guitar to his saxophone, which is wrapped in neon lights. His tunes get Mum and me instantly onto the dance floor. Dad is usually a reluctant dancer but, encouraged by the wine, he has tied his bright pink tie around his head and is throwing himself about enthusiastically. Only Grandma remains alone at the table. I put out my arms, take her hands in mine and pull her towards us. The whole family is here, dancing beneath the stars, my Grandma, my parents, my brother and his beautiful wife. It is utterly magical and somewhat surreal.

## *Chapter 47*

The summer vacation is over, and I am back at work. It is going surprisingly well. In terms of my sight, I managed to read an entire book at the end of summer, and now I can read both my phone and my computer screen. I cannot cycle into university as I used to, but instead am walking each day. It is just under three miles, so I am listening to dramas on my phone to keep things interesting. I am able to complete all of my work-related admin, keeping my nose fairly squashed up to my new, large computer screen, but the best bit is spending time with my work colleagues.

The work of a university lecturer involves not only teaching but also research. This week I have published an article in *The Conversation*, entitled "Keeping honeybees does not save bees or the environment." It is inspired by my research in Sinai, where there has been a recent increase in beekeeping. The intention is for local people to make money from the honey, but in terms of conservation the honeybees are competing with the wild bees and are reducing visitation rates to rare Sinai flowers that are found nowhere else. Here in the UK, our media often praises honeybees, as if keeping them will benefit pollination, but the reality is that they often have a negative impact on our two hundred and fifty species of wild bees, by foraging on the limited shared flowers and passing on disease. The way I put it, is that beekeeping is the equivalent of farming chickens to conserve wild birds. Beekeeping is great for producing delicious honey but keeping the domesticated honeybee has no beneficial effect on the conservation of wild bees.

In this afternoon's departmental meeting I keep peeking at my phone beneath my desk. I have tweeted my article, and it has already got over two hundred likes and a hundred retweets. Normally, I never get this much attention on twitter. Things get even more exciting when I learn that the article has made it to the national news. I hope the media will gain a little insight into the correct way of reporting honeybees in bee conservation news. My phone is running low on battery, so I put it back in my bag and start trying to concentrate. Once the meeting ends, my colleagues and I all head over to the pub, getting a long table in the garden, perfect for enjoying the evening sunlight. There is a big group of both staff and PhD students, all brilliant friends who I missed while I was in Bristol recovering from my surgery.

I sit next to Joe, a colleague who has done a lot of research in the rainforests of Brazil. He is slim, with long, twisted hair and bright, inquisitive eyes. We wrote a grant application together last year and he helped a lot when I was struggling. Grants are long and hard to write, and I had terrible headaches at the time, having to sleep with a cold, wet flannel on my forehead to reduce the pain. Tonight, Joe is asking me about my neuralgia, the twinges that are running up and down my swollen face. He reaches out and strokes my cheek. It tingles and I gaze at the smile on his handsome face.

The tingle reminds me of my first boyfriend, James, who I met in Namibia. I had sat close by him, beneath an acacia tree and offered him Zam-Buk cream for his dry lips. As he reached out our fingers had touched, tingled, and sparkled, and our eyes had met. We got together soon after that. It is not going to happen with Joe; he is taken and has a long-term partner.

The sun begins to set, but we stay and have another beer to celebrate my article. It is past eleven when I make it home. I climb straight into bed, plugging in my phone and curling up beneath my duvet. My phone rings. It is the police.

"Is that Olivia Norfolk?" the officer enquires.

"Yes..." I respond, feeling puzzled.

"This is Cambridgeshire Police. Please could you confirm your whereabouts," she follows.

"Um, yes, I am at home, in bed."

"Okay, your parents have been trying to contact you all evening. Could you confirm why they could not," she asks.

"My phone had run out of battery! Nothing serious," I tell her, wrapping up the conversation.

I ring Mum to tell her that I am safe, and that my phone had run out of battery because my article had got so many tweets. I have just been out celebrating, so it is not an occasion to call the police.

A similar thing happened in Sinai. I had emailed my parents to let them know I would be uncontactable while I spent three nights up in the mountains. Mum had promised to contact me when I got back. I had a lovely trip and, on my return to camp, kept checking my emails for her message. I got nothing and was feeling quite miffed when Kevin came up to me, in his dirty T-shirt and with his scruffy, brown hair.

"Olivia, your mother is really worried about you. You need to contact her," Kevin said.

It turned out that she had emailed Francis, my PhD supervisor in Nottingham, expressing concern about my mountain trip and wanting to check on my health and safety. I did not speak to Francis often at the time, so he had contacted Kevin over social media to find out how I was. It was humiliating, as is this call from the police, but it is good that my dear mother cares.

# Chapter 48

I cannot see perfectly, but the brain surgery went relatively well, enabling me to walk to work and do my job. In terms of future medical care, my oncologist has suggested that I could just get regular MRI scans to monitor any future changes in my tumour, or I could opt for intervention now and pursue active radiotherapy to try to halt its growth. I am keen to go ahead with active treatment if I can, because the thought of this already enormous tumour getting bigger fills me with fear. She has suggested that I have newly developed proton therapy in the place of conventional radiotherapy. In proton therapy, beams of protons are used instead of high energy X-rays. Less radiation is delivered to healthy tissue around the target site, while a higher dose is delivered to the tumour itself, enabling better focus on the tumour and less damage to the surrounding tissue.

It is not possible to have proton therapy in the UK. Although centres are being developed at two hospitals in London and Manchester, they will not open until well into next year. I want the treatment as soon as possible to stop my tumour growing. To do that, I am going to have to travel to either Switzerland or the USA. The NHS does not routinely pay the costs of travelling for this treatment, but there is a national panel that considers patients on a case-by-case basis. An application is being made on my behalf and the necessary forms have been filled in and submitted. My oncologist thinks that I have a good chance of winning the funding. It is usually awarded to children with cancer, but I am at high risk because I had radiotherapy as a baby. It damaged the surrounding tissue enough to cause the growth of my brain tumour and further radiotherapy increases the chance of more brain damage and other secondary tumours. I would really benefit from focused proton therapy that lowers this risk.

I do not know when the proton therapy will start, or where it will be. We have submitted all the application forms and have already been waiting months with no word. Things are fine here in Cambridge, but I really want to get treatment started as soon as possible. I hope it is not due to tumour growth, but I am starting to get blurred central vision, with an indistinct network of veins floating in front of everything I see.

I have booked an appointment with my consultant neuro-ophthalmologist to address my visual change. I hope it is swelling that can be reduced using steroids, but it could be tumour growth. My parents are away on holiday, so Fran comes with me to the appointment. Although she is told that it is not allowed, she nonetheless records the appointment secretly on her phone to send across to my parents. The consultant appears frustrated as she thinks that my tumour is now pressing on my optic nerve even though my neurosurgeon disagrees as he believes he removed all the tumour from around the nerve. I feel as though she takes her frustration out on me. I talk to her about the potential of swelling being the cause of my visual loss. Though she thinks I am talking nonsense, I do get prescribed dexamethasone, a potent steroid, at the end of the appointment. This will reduce any potential swelling around my tumour.

I have started taking the steroid tablets but have not noticed any improvement. If anything, my vision has got flashier, and my mind now seems super-focused. I have decided to book an appointment with a private consultant in London to get a second opinion and for my problem to be taken seriously. This time Beth comes with me, helping me find the hospital. The doctor is a delight, listening to all my symptoms and allowing me to talk for over an hour. I start to cry when I describe my loss of vision, and Beth sits at the back of the room sharing my pain. The consultant is very empathic but at the end of the consultation she simply agrees with the proposed upcoming proton therapy and has no other suggestions of how to improve things. Afterwards, Beth and I head to Granary Square, close to Kings Cross railway station. We sit outside in the glorious sunshine, eating focaccia and drinking rosé wine. Beth's long brown hair glistens in the light and she looks beautiful. There may not be any obvious answers about how to save my health, but I am lucky to have such wonderful friends who are happy to help me on my journey.

I am starting to feel a little too buzzy, or manic, which I think maybe a side-effect of the steroids. I ring the secretary of my neuro-ophthalmologist to ask if I should stop or reduce my dose, and she refers me to my oncologist. It turns out that the oncologist is on holiday for two weeks and I am advised to continue taking the steroids until she returns. I do as they tell me, just hoping that the medication helps bring back my sight. My parents have heard what is happening to me, about my drugs and my visual change, so they decide to cut their holiday short. They fly back to England and come to take me back to Bristol.

The mental buzzing is getting stronger, as if the steroids are releasing my brain from all the pressure created by my tumour. I ring my brother to explain what is going on. My speech is quick and rushed. I tell him how the steroids have cleared my tiredness and seem to have brought me a new life. I feel saved.

My brother does not share my feelings. He phones my parents immediately.

"Olivia has become manic; she needs to reduce her dose of dexamethasone," Tim says in a serious tone.

He does not share my enthusiasm for the recent changes in my wellbeing. He is worried about me and insists that we should seek medical help.

Oh, I love my brother, but he does not understand how everything in the world is getting better.


## Chapter 49


I am wide awake.

Everyone else is asleep. We had Fran with us for dinner. She and my parents went to bed hours ago. I am still sitting at the kitchen table. At first, I had been planning my new bathroom, but now my mind is racing. I know it is the steroids, but I must get my thoughts written down. I must tell my story. My brain has never felt this alive; my ideas have never been so clear. The words are cascading from my fingertips, the sentences arriving fully formed on my laptop screen. I must get it all written down before dawn.

My life story pours out of me as soon as the realisation hits me.

"I can see the bigger picture now. This is not just about me. It is about all of us."

I hurriedly open a blank document and begin typing.

"This time I will write something of real importance. I will write the book to save humanity.

"From the perspective of my loved ones, I know it seems that I have gone mad. Remember I am on high dose steroids which are making me hyper, but my thoughts and the words I am writing are not incoherent.

"My brain tumour has been growing silently throughout most of my adult life. I only realise this now that the swelling has shifted, and I have experienced this incredible lightness of body and mind.

"Looking back the signs were obvious. My migraines worsening, my balance faltering, the fatigue creeping into my life. And then the blindness. The changes were gradual, but why did I not recognise them?

"Because my body has been adapting. As my reserves weakened, my subconscious brain has been learning and prioritising the behaviours that are essential for happiness, discarding actions that cost energy and bring no reward. My brain has learnt to distract me from its decay by only performing tasks that bring me joy.

"Last January the headaches were crippling. I slept with a damp cloth on my forehead. Yet in between the hours of sleep, I felt the need to run, to take up yoga. Even in the face of crushing pain these activities are worth it, the endorphins and sense of peace necessary for creating the illusion of wellbeing.

"The activities in the year before the darkness were selected to bring me maximum happiness. Most of these things are obvious, backed up by science, but my brain has catalogued them all in one place, and it is my duty to share what I have learned with the wider world. I am not writing about saving the world because I am deluded about my powers, nor because I think I have been sent here by God. This is all beyond my control, a true miracle of nature."

I stop for a moment.

"I suddenly realise the broader implications. I have not been in control of my life. Free will was just an illusion. My brain has been filtering my actions, only allowing me to perform tasks that may benefit our species. As a teenager I planned to become a medical doctor, but I was side-tracked by what I discovered during my art A-level. I studied the form of animals, observing their life-force, realising we are all part of nature, we are all one and the same. As I painted the eyes of an elephant who was wise beyond my years, my brain was sealing my fate. I had to save our wildlife, find a solution to our collapsing ecosystems. I did not choose my path, it chose me. The earth is in crisis and despite my limited brain activity I have to try to find a solution. Not for me, not for humanity, but for the survival of everything we know."

My mind is whirling faster now. I am scared and confused.

"It cannot be down to me to fix this. Yet all the information I have ever learnt about sustainability is bubbling to the surface, neurons firing incessantly in a desperate bid to find the solution."

My thoughts keep circling.

"Something does not make sense. Something is missing. Round and round, the cogs whirring faster and faster, a machine that is set to explode.

"Eureka!"

The apple hits me hard on the head. Before I know it, my legs are running up the stairs and I find myself banging on my parents' bedroom door.

"I have finally found the missing link. The final piece of the colossal jigsaw that is life on earth. The answer to the universal question. The key which will unlock the theory of everything and guarantee the survival of life on earth.

"Time. It is not continuous. It can curve, it can bend, it can loop," I cry.

I am not typing anymore. My manic thoughts are getting faster and pouring straight from my mouth

"What we do now is connected to then, to past, to future. I am the butterfly who flaps its wings and changes everything. A cascade of impacts moving through space and time, changing the world. What I write, what I say, what I decide will affect the very future of humanity. Whether we adapt or whether we die. How many starve and how many thrive. Will we all love or will we all cry?

"If I find myself moving through time, I know the world will treat me as mad. I will be locked up. I will be isolated. I will be alone. I will die.

"I need help to get through this.

"Promise to trust me. Promise to always tell the truth. Promise to write down the words of my story," I say with desperation.

"Promise not to leave me alone. Promise to touch me before leaving me.

"This is important. I do not know why. Human touch keeps us grounded. Keeps us safe. Keeps us loved."

Dad holds my arms and promises to do it all. I hope it will keep me safe.

The thoughts continue cascading from my mind. I go on to describe the meaning of the entire planet, the human race, why we exist, what we must do to be happy, what we must do to survive.

I do not know whether Dad can understand what I am saying, I am not sure that the sounds can be heard as words. It may sound like I am speaking in tongues, as if I am overcome by religious rapture, but in my head I am telling the story of my life; these are the words of the novel I plan to write.

I must be dying. There is no other explanation. The swelling must have become too much, the pressure on my brain reaching the limit. Yet everything that is happening to me is so familiar. The eureka moment, that epiphany when all your thoughts suddenly collide and make the bigger picture clear has been spoken of by so many other scientists. If it happened to them, maybe it could happen to me. Maybe this was a physiological phenomenon, rare, but one which could be survived. One that could secure me a place in history.

"I do not want to be famous.

"If it is down to me to save the world, I cannot bear the responsibility What if I make a mistake? What if my decisions cause others pain or suffering? The answers can never be decided by one individual. They must be adaptable, responsive to science, to evidence and to reason."

This I decide is the key to our planet's survival.

"But the key to human survival is something else. It is love."

With that thought, my words gather speed. My brain recalls all those that have loved me in my life, all those that I have loved. I start with the obvious, with my parents, Guy and Selena, my brother Tim, and my grandparents, Donald and Margaret, and Louise, and then my aunts and uncles, Ali and Neil, Carole and Steve, Clio, and Mel and Pete. The list spirals out of control, moving on to my cousins and then friends from school, from university, followed by my PhD, Sinai, Romania, York, and Cambridge. The list does not stop. I also recite the names of all those who have helped make me who I am, those who have shaped my knowledge and understanding of the world. Beginning with Francis Gilbert and Marcus Echhorn, my PhD supervisors, and then going back in time all the way to Miss Hewish, my first primary school teacher. And everyone else.

"The names of all of you that I have met come out one by one, because I am thankful to you all. Because I love you."

Finally, after what feels like an eternity the words slow to a trickle. The names run out. I collapse on the bed.

"This must be it. Death."

I am lying on my back, too weak to move. I try to draw a breath. My nose is blocked, my throat closed, and in this position, little gets through into my airways. I feel a colossal weight pressing down on me, a desperate need for air. I begin to panic, but then I see it, the white light. It is luminescent, brighter than any star. It draws me in. The glow dissolving all my pain and fear, filling me with a euphoria unlike anything I felt when I was alive. It offers release as I float towards it.

I feel my dad's hand on my shoulder, his care and tenderness pull me back from the brink. I do not want to leave him. I do not want to die. Instead, my body shudders as I gasp desperately for one more breath. Mum has wrapped herself in her dressing gown and gone downstairs to call for help. Dad remains next to me, holding me, child-like, in his embrace and stroking me gently as I try to breathe.

Thick mucus is building up in the back of my throat, tar-like. I need to cough, but my body fails to cooperate. I feel the panic begin to rise once again.

"I need to breathe. I cannot breathe. I cannot. White, transcendent light."

The white hole has re-emerged in front of me, that euphoric high, tempting me to fly upwards and leave this useless body below. I start moving towards it, willing to leave, but once again I feel Dad's hand stroking my hair and I am pulled back by the power of his love, forcing me to cough and splutter. It goes on for hours and I begin to register the voices on the bedside radio. The news stories keep flipping, positive to negative, each time I come back. Switching from the negativity of Boris, the Brexiteers, and their harsh words about the EU towards environmentalism and the ways to improve our world. It feels like even the news is in a time loop.

Eventually I leave my parent's bed and go downstairs, where the world continues in its time loop. When I am with my mum things slow down a bit and I can rest. We can chat at a normal pace. She walks me around the garden, letting me stroke the flowers that I can no longer see.

When I am with Dad, I talk at the speed of light, the words to the books I need to write gushing from my mouth with little time to stop and think. I hope he is writing it all down, but I suspect I am too fast.

"There are so many books to compose. First, I need to finish the story of my life in Sinai. I have the ending. I am standing alone with my beautiful colleague, Joe. We are both posing on one leg in the yoga tree position, beneath an exquisite rainbow that we once saw arcing across the sky high above the glistening sea on the deer-filled Isle of Rum. It is the perfect ending, full of happiness and joy."

I move on, still speaking uncontrollably to my dad. Next is an environmental book, about the ways we need to change to make the planet sustainable. About how we need to regenerate farming. How we can use agroforestry to enhance ecosystem services such as nutrient-fixing and pollination, so that we can produce sustainable food in the future.

It is late afternoon and I shift onto my third book, realising that a key aspect of sustainability is how we treat one another.

"We need to champion equality, treating people from different genders and races with equal respect. We need to tackle issues about disability, ensuring that societies look after all without discrimination, treating the disabled well and never talking down to them.

"Ah, I know what I must do. I must create a new stone tablet to rival the ten commandments of Moses. I know the stone mason. I will ask him to carve the key principles underpinning my perfect world on a rock that we can place at the top of Hamza's mountain in Fox Camp. I am still thinking of all the elements necessary, but for now the tablet should say:

1. Love
2. Truth
3. Understanding.

# Chapter 50

The ambulance pulls into our drive. I am lying on my back on the sitting room floor, once again struggling to breathe. The paramedics come in and start discussing my symptoms with my parents, ignoring me completely. I can no longer see. I have decided to judge people by their politeness, and these people are being rude.

A decision is made to take me to the Accident & Emergency department. The paramedics lead me out to their ambulance. Dad sits with me in the back while Mum follows us in her car. At the hospital, I am placed on a hospital trolley and put into an outside queue. Dad tries to calm me and explains what is going on. Mum soon joins us and in due course we are taken into the A&E department and placed in a cubicle.

Eventually I am seen by a doctor. He thinks that I am probably suffering from steroid-induced psychosis but wants a CT scan of my head to ensure there hasn't been a new development with my tumour. The scan shows no new complications. Conversations are held with my oncologist in Cambridge and the outcome is that I am advised to stop taking the steroids. Usually, they advise patients to come off steroids slowly because stopping suddenly can cause damage to the adrenal glands. But, in view of the severity of my psychosis, they think I should stop immediately. I haven't slept for forty-eight hours so I am also prescribed a strong tranquiliser to calm me down and help me sleep.

We leave A&E and head to the car, which is parked down a narrow street overlooked by tall buildings. As we do so, I can suddenly see us clearly. I have what appears to be a bird's eye view of me walking between my parents, grinning in my colourful pyjamas.

Over the next couple of days, I feel calmer although I remain trapped in the time loop. I have stopped vomiting out my books when I am with Dad. Instead, we sit on the sofa chatting more coherently about the storylines, allowing him to write down details of the plots.

I spend time with Mum watching Les Misérables, explaining to her how breathing out the music creates the song of death, which is something I had never noticed before. At other times I dance to music from around the world, letting my body move frenetically and free. I also perform yoga for hours, stretching into positions that my body appears to cry out for. In the past, I have danced in clubs and at weddings, and have done yoga in class, but now I feel totally in tune with my body and let it move with its own life.

I start struggling to decide what to eat. My body seems to call out for what it wants, sandwiches, fish, fruit. I cannot see well enough to find the food I need in our kitchen so start asking my parents to feed me. I have decided to write my next book about nutrition. I know little about it, but it is at the heart of a sustainable future.

"We need to reduce the amount of meat we eat. We do not all need to become vegetarians, meat just needs to be something we eat on special occasions, not every day. It produces so much more carbon than vegetables. Modern-day farming is also terrible, causing real distress for our livestock. We need to be kind to all animals on this planet. We also must not over-harvest wild plants. Fungi. Animals. Fish. Shellfish. We must not drive them extinct. We must save our biodiversity."

Things keep spinning.

My nutrition is becoming imbalanced. I need to go back to hospital so they can test my blood and identify the problem. I do not think my parents will listen to me. They think I am mad. I do not know what to do.

"I need to get an ambulance. Urgently. Perhaps I could leap in front of a car speeding down the lane. I could break a leg. But what if the driver was harmed? I don't want that."

And then. The solution.

I will jump out of my parent's window. Attempt suicide. I am sure dad will pull me in and save me."

I run upstairs, screaming to get my parents' attention. I feel my way to their window, open it and crawl out onto the ledge. I cannot see anything but hold on to the window frame with one arm. Then I let go, allowing myself to fall backwards. I am entirely serious. But Dad had heard my screams and had rushed up to the bedroom. As I released my grip on the window frame he grabs my arm, clinging on and pulling me back into the room.

The police are called. I am a danger to myself. Then paramedics. I am very suspicious of the male paramedic but the female police officer coaxes me into the ambulance.

I am back in hospital once again, lying on a bed in the observation room in the A&E department. There is a man in the bed next to me. He is grunting. It is clear that he is masturbating, and I shout out telling him to stop. I explain to my parents that men must be more polite around women, but they tell me that he is ill and wearing a breathing machine.

"Oh, I am so sorry, I hope you get well soon," I say, facing his direction.

I have blood tests and another CT scan of my head before being admitted to the Acute Medical Unit. I remember being admitted to the ward, and running to the tap, downing water as if I was dying of thirst. Once my desire for fluids is satisfied, I experience extreme hunger, and start stuffing down hospital sandwiches. I continue pestering my parents to get me extra food, salty smoked salmon sandwiches and sushi. I am sure they will make my body better.

My memory of events then starts to fade away. Everything becomes a blur and I remember very little about the next three days in Bristol. I think I remained pretty manic, demanding that my mattress be removed from my bed and placed on the floor. There, I sat playing a makeshift drum, turning over a plastic waste-bin and bashing out the *Sa'idi* rhythm. After that I think I grew very weary and started to fall asleep.

Now I am lying in an ambulance with my mum by my side. We are being transferred to Addenbrookes Hospital in Cambridge. It is a five-hour trip. They are moving me to see my neurosurgeon to get advice about my vision. It has become even worse. My left eye is bulging out of its socket and I can see hardly anything now. I have also developed what they call visual snow. My visual field is completely taken over by tiny, multi-coloured, sparkling and flickering dots, as if I am gazing up at a clear sky, filled with a billion stars.

## Chapter 51

An enormous elephant is strolling towards me across the vast savannah, and around its feet dozens of antelope are frolicking. My brother has explained that I am suffering from Charles Bonnet syndrome, where the brains of the severely visually impaired imagine things. It is a fake world that I am seeing around me. But I do not want to get confused, so I instruct my mind to see fish and an underwater community instead. This way I will know it is not real because I am currently confined to a bed in the High Dependency Unit where I am aware that I am neither wet nor submerged.

When I arrived back at Addenbrookes Hospital I had blood tests immediately. I have severe hyponatraemia, a potentially life-threatening condition brought on by very low blood salt levels. The low sodium levels are responsible for my profound sleepiness and have made my brain swollen and oedematous. They suspect that the hyponatraemia may have been caused by the anti-psychotics I was prescribed in Bristol, but they can't be sure because no-one checked my blood while I was an in-patient there.

My neurosurgeon comes and leans over me. The fish have disappeared and now I can see his face. He suggests that I have more surgery to remove tumour from my optic nerve to try to save my sight. I disagree. The surgery created so much swelling and took months to heal last time and I don't want to undergo that ordeal again. Plus, I think that my vision is improving.

My parents and brother are concerned that my psychosis is not yet fully resolved, and I may not have the mental capacity to make important decisions about my future. My brother stands next to me and insists on testing my vision in front of the consultant. He waves his hands in my face and asks me if I can see them. I cannot. The images of the doctor are entirely imagined.

My decision not to have further surgery is respected. After two days on the High Dependency Unit my sodium levels have started to improve, and I am moved into a single room on the general neurosurgery ward. The senior nurse assigned to me is a Filipino who treats me kindly, chatting about how I feel and about the world around us. This is how it should be done.

I am discharged from hospital four-days later and allowed to return home. Now I start to acknowledge my blindness, meeting Helena, a lovely woman from the council who starts training me to use a white cane. As I talk with her about preparing for a life without sight, I begin to realise that

I should have been registered as severely visually impaired since the days after my surgery. I had no idea. I could have accessed so much additional support when I returned to work. I had not appreciated that ninety per cent of people who are considered blind can actually see a blurred version of their surroundings.

I go to CamSight, a Cambridge based charity for those with visual impairment, and meet Jerry, their technology man. Although he is totally blind, I can now see a little movement so am able to reach out and shake his proffered hand. He teaches me about the narrating software available on my phone and computer. If I want to keep working, I need to learn how to use it, and how to touch type. It is a perfect mission for me to tackle while we are away for my proton therapy.

There have been repeated delays in gaining approval for my treatment, during which time my tumour has grown and is now partially blocking my nasal airways, causing difficulty with breathing. It is now nearly six months, but at last we have a date to go to Jacksonville in Florida where I will get two months of proton therapy.

My vision has improved a little since the hyponatraemia and mentally I am in a better place. Apart from today.

We are back in Bristol before flying out to the States. It is bonfire night, and I am sitting at the kitchen table when everything slips out of place.

"I am giving birth!" I cry, as I suddenly feel horrendous cramps and know that I am in labour.

Dad takes me next door and makes me lie down, as if I was one of his patients. He presses on my stomach, feeling for a pregnant womb, reassuring me that there is nothing there. I am comforted and the pains disappear. I return to the kitchen, but the time loop is back and flips things over. The contractions return.

Whose baby could it be? I have not had sex for nine months. I do not believe that I am the new Mary. This is not a virgin birth.

Dad could have raped me in the night, but I know he wouldn't do that.

And then the realisation.

Oh, it could be Joe's. We have not had sex, but we could have it in the future. I can show that it is our baby using DNA tests, and then we can fall in love and look after our child."

I so want this to be true, but Joe has a long-term partner, they love each other, and she would be crushed if this all came true.

I cannot do that to her. I leave the room, moving alone to my bedroom and lying down. Here I am on a different timeline and the labour stops. I shut my eyes and fall asleep. I dream of being with Joe and having his child.

A week later I fly out to Florida with Dad. I have not escaped the time loop and he is understanding as I explain that my actions can influence the future of our world. As we sit in the airport, a call goes out over the Tannoy speaker for someone who speaks Arabic. I nearly go, thinking I could help someone get on the plane. But then I imagine that my behaviour might provoke some terrorist incident, so I decide to stay where I am.

Our flight is delayed and we are instructed to move to a different departure lounge. Everybody moves from their chairs, standing up and congregating in a crowd around the new gate. I insist that we should all stay where we are, sitting on the comfortable, empty seats instead of standing in line for an hour. Dad laughs and agrees with my point but pulls me up and drags me towards the back of the queue.

The flight is uneventful, and we arrive in Jacksonville for the first time. We are taken by taxi to a car rental centre where Dad takes charge of the rental car that has been provided for us during our stay. We drive to our accommodation, a ground-floor flat in a complex with a swimming pool and gym. It should be lovely, but as he walks me around the site all I can feel is swathes of concrete and all I can hear is the noisy and busy state highway that runs alongside the complex.

I miss home.

## Chapter 52

We have to wait one week before going to the Proton Centre. It is a modern, private hospital built about two hundred yards away from a much larger public hospital. Entering the Centre, we find ourselves in an enormous, bright atrium, where we are greeted by a friendly and helpful receptionist. We are directed to comfortable seating where patients and their relatives wait before the patients are taken through locked doors for their treatment. There is a large grand piano in the centre of the atrium, on which patients, both past and present, play music to soothe and comfort those undergoing treatment for a variety of different cancers. We are invited to help ourselves to free coffee, cookies and doughnuts that are available every day.

After a short wait we are taken through to meet the nursing team, who weigh and measure me, and record my wellbeing out a score of ten. This has never been done by the NHS.

In the days that follow, I learn that when the proton therapy takes place it is vital that my head is in precisely the same position every day. This will be achieved by placing a personalised mask over my head and screwing it down to the treatment table. Today, two women greet me and explain how they are going to create this mask. I must take my top off because it will interfere with their work.

"Oh my God, I love your bra," one of them cries.

"It is an amazing colour," shrieks the other, as I stand in nothing but my bright pink bralette.

When I lie down, they start stroking my hair, saying that it needs to be put in pigtails that will not get in the way. Once they have done my make over, they begin, rubbing the wet plaster all over my face. They poke a tube through to my mouth for me to breathe through and it takes nearly half an hour for them to finish. They peel off the mask, freeing me, and things are over for the day.

I have to undergo further MRI scans so the physicists can model the irradiation fields. It is important that they ensure the whole of my complex shaped tumour is included while protecting surrounding vital structures as much as possible. It all takes time, and my treatment doesn't start until the third week of my stay in Florida.

The plan is to undergo proton therapy for a total of eight weeks. There are three proton machines at the Centre, each supported by a large gantry, each assigned a colour, blue, green, or yellow. Five times a week we are telephoned to be told what colour gantry we have been assigned to that day and what time the day's treatment is scheduled. The times can range from first thing in the morning to early evening. We are normally a twenty-minute drive away from the Centre but at rush hour the five-lane state highway becomes gridlocked, and we have to time our departures carefully to ensure we don't miss our treatment slot.

On day one we are assigned the three o-clock slot in the afternoon. Mum flew out to join us last week and both my parents accompany me to the appointment. We sit in the airy atrium waiting to be called. Often there are problems with the machines and waits can be quite long. Jigsaws are provided to help people while away the time, and a paint therapist is on hand most days to support patients and their carers. Several of the patients are young children with cancer and the therapist is popular with them.

On this occasion I only have to wait about twenty minutes before being called. I am escorted by one of the radiographers to the gantry where I lie on the treatment table and have my head pinned down using the fibreglass mask created for me earlier. Then the table moves and treatment begins. There is a constant, guttural whirring that lasts for thirty minutes as the protons are fired at my tumour. The radiographers suggest that I create a playlist of music to fill the time and block out the noise of the machine.

The treatment makes my face tingle. When we get back to our apartment, I hold a refrigerated can of beer against my prickling skin before cracking it open to drink. The Centre feels like a great place, but this is going to be a long two months.

The following day, I listen to my own music during treatment. The spirituality of Bob Marley's lyrics makes the experience less uncomfortable. Back at the apartment we have little to do. As the days begin to roll by, we feel increasingly claustrophobic. Mum starts to go out for walks, taking note of the birds around her. I try to fill my time using the blind typing software, but this infuriates me because I keep getting everything wrong. Most days I go to the gym with Dad, where he helps me onto one of the exercise bikes. It helps burn off my stress but there is so much time to fill it seems unbearable.

As we never know what time I am needed for proton therapy, it is hard to plan things to do outside of the flat in advance. On some days we do manage to get out though, driving to the coast and walking through the mangrove forest or the oyster middens where the soil has been created from ancient piles of used oyster shells. The paths are bumpy and particularly hard for blind people to navigate. Dad finds a stick and holds it out for me. I can see nothing of the forest floor, so just trust him and follow his brightly coloured T-shirt, feeling changes in direction and incline through the stick.

We also visit the immaculate Florida beaches, where I can just about make out the pale, white sand which stretches out endlessly alongside the blue sea. We walk until we are tired, and then turn back the way we came. It feels beautiful, but I want to run along the beach feeling the sand between my toes. I try, but it is so difficult. I wish I could see more.

Days become weeks. Nothing changes. The smiling, over-weight, middle-aged security guard is still sitting in the foyer of the Centre beneath a sign politely proclaiming, "No guns allowed". Each day we laugh about the fact that we could run faster than him.

All the staff are kind and friendly. The identities of the radiographers escorting me to the therapy room change day-by-day. As they guide me, we chat, and I hear about their weekend or about their life. Some seem a little bit depressed and ready for change. Many of them have moved far from their homes to find work at the Centre and they seem lonely.

Waiting in the atrium for my treatment becomes more challenging. Mum doesn't want to drive over here so Dad brings me for treatment every day. He usually sits waiting patiently, reading a voluminous biography of Churchill that he brings with him. Mum accompanies us most days. She begins going out for walks around the hospital complex, drawing expressions of concern from patients who know the area and consider it a far too poor and dangerous neighbourhood for her to be walking around alone. Sometimes she fills in the time with the jigsaw puzzle or the art activity table. I joined it once, drawing my visual experience of the world, a series of thin, wiggly lines and star-like dots. The art therapist tried to chat to me about it. Her positivity was infuriating and drove me mad. I scribbled across my artwork to represent the final stage of visual darkness, crumpled it up and threw it in her direction. When I sat down with my parents I felt some relief, reflecting that the therapy may have made me feel better.

The Centre closes for two-days over Christmas and we decide to drive down the coast to spend the time being pampered in a fancy hotel. My parents describe to me an enormous, almost life-sized pirate ship made of gingerbread that is filling up the entrance hall. The hotel is serving a festive menu on Christmas Eve. There is no roast turkey with all the trimmings on Christmas Day itself. Instead, we have delicious, freshly prepared sushi and cocktails for our Christmas meal. Mum and I have booked a massage for after lunch. The masseurs are both male and I feel nervous as I undress, climbing naked into a towel-covered bed. My masseur enters; he is big and bearded. He seems to be smiling as he approaches me. We begin talking as he kneads away the tension in my back. He begins telling me about his life, how he used to be a rodeo-rider who was once thrown from his bull. The fall had numbed the entire right-side of his body, forcing him to learn how to write and function with his left hand. Given time, the numbness had gone away, so now he is ambidextrous, able to use both hands equally well. It helped when he massaged, he explained. I understood what he meant. He was amazing, both his hands sensing my tension and massaging it away, melting it like butter. After the hour I felt rejuvenated.

The Centre also closes for two-days over the New Year. We decide to celebrate New Year's Eve at the apartment. The three of us sit outside on our small terrace. It is dark and all

I can hear is the noise of traffic on the highway, but this does not dampen our celebrations. Dad has brought me a large celebratory cigar. At midnight I take a sip of my Jack Daniels and inhale on the cigar. As I blow out the heavy smoke, I lean back on my chair and grin.

It has not been the best year,
but I do have the best parents.

## 2019

*With mum in Jacksonville*

# Chapter 53

The New Year has not brought good tidings. The cornea of my eye has become red and inflamed. I have been referred to a local optician who initially prescribed eye drops. These have not helped so he has now suggested that I try to protect the eye by wearing a new type of contact lens that can be worn continuously, both day and night, for over a week at a time. I thought it was worth a try, not least because it would be more sustainable if everyone switched from daily disposable contact lenses to this option. But secretly, as I had requested an optically corrected lens, I was hoping that I would notice positive changes to my vision.

The contact lens did not improve my vision, nor did it protect my eye. It is becoming increasingly painful, so we have been sent to the Emergency Room at the public hospital to obtain an ophthalmological opinion. It is right next door to the Proton Centre, but the whole experience is completely different. It is clear that the gulf between private and public medicine is immense. The public hospital also has a polite notice advising, "No guns allowed", but here the security guards are armed and have the physiques of beefed-up nightclub bouncers. Before we can enter the ER reception, we have to go through airport type security, passing through a metal detector and then being frisked.

After being examined by an ER physician we are taken into the hospital to be seen by the on-call consultant ophthalmologist. We are given seats in a long corridor outside the consulting room. As we sit waiting to be seen, I see people shuffling past me and can make out the colour of bright orange. It is a line of prisoners, shackled together with a chain that links heavy metal cuffs on both their hands and feet. Apparently, they are all black men. It is abhorrent. In the UK, prisoners in hospital only ever have handcuffs and a member of prison staff leading the way. Here there are echoes of the slave trade. It really needs to change.

In time, I am seen by the ophthalmologist. He tells me that I have a serious corneal ulcer and there is a risk that the eyeball may perforate if it is not treated effectively. He prescribes antibiotic eye drops and tells me that it is essential they are applied every thirty minutes, day and night.

We have been in the hospital for just under eight hours by the time the consultation is over and it is 10.30 p.m. As we prepare to leave, a nurse comes to warn us that there has been some gun activity outside the hospital. A man has mugged one of her colleagues, shoving a gun in her face. We are advised that it is unsafe to walk through the carpark to our car unaccompanied and that we should wait until a security guard is available to drive us in his van. We realise that this is such a different country to our own and so say yes to the lift. It is dark and raining outside. When the guard arrives, we squeeze into the front of his small van and are driven the short distance to our car.

Dad drives us back. En route my parents discuss how they are going to apply my drops. They decide to split the schedule during the night, with one staying up until four o'clock before swapping with the other and getting the chance to get some sleep. Mum sets the timer of her watch to thirty-minute intervals to wake whichever of them is on duty. It is horrible. It feels like torture. I lie in bed, trying to sleep, but every half an hour one of them comes into my bedroom, prises my eyelids apart, and squirts drops into my painful, red eye.

As the nights pass, I become exhausted, never able to sleep for more than half an hour. My parents are also getting tired. Mum has started watching ad-free tv, public service broadcasting that is showing night-time opera, Orpheus and Eurydice, which keeps her going between applications of the drops.

By day I still have my proton therapy, and there is no chance to relax or do other things. On the positive side, my eye is beginning to improve. The redness and pain have gone down, but I am so tired.

The drops are nearly finished, and once they are, I am at last able to sleep heavily. It is a wondrous release from the torture of the previous seven days. My parents are also glad to sleep but they feel guilty about what they have had to inflict on me. Dad takes hold of my shoulders and starts a gentle, restorative massage by way of an apology. It is lovely. My parents have started to encourage massage; it is a good way to interact and connect with a needy, blind person, and is something I have never thought of trying before I lost my sight.

When we were visiting St Augustin, the oldest town in America, they suggested I give reflexology a try. And so it was that I found myself being guided down a dark staircase into a gloomy room, decorated with flecks of gold. A Chinese man greeted me and escorted me to a soft chair, where he massaged my feet for half an hour. He was squeezing my feet and prodding between my toes, but it was magic. I felt the tension in my shoulders melting away, and bizarrely I felt my mucus-filled sinuses clearing.

When we got home, Dad started reading the science associated with reflexology, learning that it can be effective in promoting deep relaxation and wellbeing. Different points on the feet are said to correspond to different parts of the body and he tries to learn these, studying the images and using my foot as a blank canvas. He does get pretty good but is no match for the skilled Chinese professional.

As another way of relaxing, I have also started playing my flute. I am now no longer able to read music and to start with it is infuriating, having to play tunes by ear or by memory. But in time I get the hang of it and manage to play traditional songs such as Amazing Grace and Auld Lang Syne quite proficiently. I find that playing without music is really satisfying for blind people like me, allowing me to play with real instinct and joy.

I have learnt to play my own compositions too. I have struggled to play anything that reminds me of the mountains in Sinai, but I have composed a piece that is inspired by where we are now. It is a slow and melancholy piece, which makes me ready to fly home. It is called:

"Jacksonville, Why Are You So Grey?"

# Chapter 54

The proton therapy is nearly over. Once a week there are lunch time sessions where patients and their carers are able to find support and solace from shared experience while enjoying a free lunch provided by the Centre and listening to a short lecture from one of the oncologists. This is representative of the very holistic approach to the treatment provided here and such is the value of the get-togethers that some past patients travel vast distances to attend the lunches. At the end of the session, patients are invited to address the fifty or sixty attendees and give testimonials about their experience. I am a lecturer who has spoken in public so many times, but today I cannot bear it. Instead, I sit nibbling my food. I cannot even taste it as the proton therapy has taken away my sense of taste. I take a big sip of wine and wish this would be over.

An old, black man stands up. He thanks the Centre for his proton therapy, talking with an extremely strong Southern American accent. He moves on, showering effusive thanks on his insurance company; without them he could not have come here. It is so different to the NHS. Next there is a well-spoken white woman, who again thanks her insurance company for agreeing to pay for her treatment. She then gives thanks to the Lord and I get a hint of what life may be like in the bible-belt of America. An English girl follows, rolling forwards in her wheelchair. She has a bald head from previous chemotherapy, and is extremely unwell, with little knowledge about whether she has been cured. She gives a beautiful speech, thanking the staff members and the Proton Centre. I am impressed. The real reason that I am reluctant to speak, is because I too do not know whether the treatment has worked.

Dad speaks on my behalf. He is a great speaker. He starts by thanking the NHS for funding my treatment, and then moves on thanking the doctors and the wonderful support staff. I look up. I agree with him totally on this. Nobody is left out. He thanks the receptionist we see every day for the warmth of her daily greetings, the art therapist and even the woman who has been running free evening yoga classes that we have attended. When he finishes, I join the room in a standing ovation.

The following day is my last day of proton therapy. I lie under the gantry, my mask screwed down to the treatment table. The staff are lovely, and the treatments have been more tolerable now I bring my own music, but I am glad that it will be over. When I am guided out to meet my parents in the atrium, I discover that a big group of staff has congregated to say goodbye, including my specialist nurse and consultant oncologist. At the Centre there is a tradition that patients ring a bell to signal the end of their treatment, surrounded by their family and cheering clinic staff. It is almost like a graduation ceremony, providing a sense of closure. When I arrived, I thought it was silly and had intended to refuse to take part, but now I have been won over.

Long chimes hang down from the atrium roof with a thick central rope reaching all the way to the floor. I feel excited as I am handed the long rope and, after a moment of fear when I am unsure quite what to do, I swing the rope and whack the bells. It makes a wonderful sound and cheers go up from the staff and other patients waiting for their treatment. Mum then joins me for photos with my oncologist and the clinic staff. Dad has disappeared. He is crying, hiding in a side-room to conceal his emotions. The art therapist has noticed and goes to offer him comfort.

We have to wait a week before we are allowed to fly home just in case there are any complications from the proton therapy that make it unsafe to fly. But at last we have packed everything up and are heading to return our hire car. My parents fill in the paperwork at the rental drop-off and we sit and wait for a taxi to take us to the airport. I hear my parents chatting with an English woman next to us. She and her family have just arrived for proton therapy. They are waiting to pick up their rental car before driving to the same apartment complex as ours. The woman and her mother-in-law sound nice and part of me thinks it is a shame we are going home and will never got to know them.

It took me a while to notice the child accompanying the two women. His name is Noah. He is two years old. He has a medulloblastoma, a malignant brain tumour, and in his short life he has already endured two brain surgeries. Now he is here for proton therapy.

"Olivia had retinoblastoma at his age," Dad says to Noah's mother. He explains, "She had radiotherapy which has led to a meningioma, which is why we are here."

"The proton therapy has been absolutely fine. Nothing to worry about," I say. "The staff will really look after you. It certainly won't be worse than the surgery he has already been through," I add.

I remember the fear I felt that first week we had arrived. It would have helped to have had someone tell me things would be alright.

Noah sounds like he is getting tired. I want to reach out to him but cannot be sure how close he is to me. Or whether he is well enough to play. His mother tells us that her husband had recently suffered from a collapsed lung. He is not allowed to fly and will not make it out here for several weeks. Her mother-in-law is here in his place. They are nervous about driving on the wrong side of the road and have heard the roads were dangerous. They are right. This proton experience is made so much harder by being in a different country, so far from home.

Noah spoke up.

"Why so long?" he asks.

He must be exhausted after his overnight flight from Manchester. We heard how the airport assistance had offered to push Noah's buggy because he qualified as disabled, but no one had helped with their heavy luggage, filled with all the medical equipment needed for his care. The journey had been a struggle.

The older woman leans over her grandson and says fondly, "You have been such a good boy, Noah. Keep being good for a while longer. We will get the hire car soon and I will take you to the shop and buy you a football."

I cannot see his face, but his voice sounds full of smiles as he replies, "Football, football, football."

Thirty years ago, I was one of the first children to have successful radiotherapy for recurrent retinoblastoma. It is a miracle that I survived. Here we are thirty years later, and everything has changed. Yet everything is the same. This child could be me, undertaking strange new treatments in an effort to save his precious life. The proton therapy should reduce his risk of developing a secondary tumour as I did, but I do hope that he receives regular follow-up scans throughout his life, just in case.

This is the new generation. It would be nice to think that baby Noah can save our planet from the coming floods caused by global warming. But at least let him have the chance to follow his dreams, play football, live, love and be free.

As I sat there waiting to go home, uncertain of my future, I felt a sudden sense of peace. It is not Noah's responsibility to save our planet from the threats of colossal loss of wildlife, climate change, and food insecurity. It is ours. I believe we do have the power to make change and am hopeful that we will do so. That by working together across continents, between cultures and generations, we can and will save the world.

# Epilogue

The proton therapy has not worked. My tumour is still growing and I am completely blind. If you can, please let me know when we will next see the blue moon. I will not be able to see the moonlight—I will just see my imaginary flickering stars—but I hope it will bring us luck. Let us build a positive future for us all.

*Olivia with her niece and nephew*

# *Afterword*
## *by*
## *Guy Norfolk (Olivia's father)*

Olivia finished writing about Noah at the end of March 2022. It had always been her intention to finish her story on this note of optimism and hope. The following is my account of what happened next.

### *2019*

Although the future is uncertain for Olivia when we fly back from Jacksonville, she has more pressing medical matters to deal with on her return to the UK. Her corneal ulcer has still not healed, so an emergency appointment is arranged for her to see a specialist at Addenbrookes Hospital in Cambridge. A week after arriving home she is undergoing urgent surgery to sew her left eyelids together with temporary stiches. It is hoped that this will protect her cornea and allow it to heal, the resultant total blindness being an unavoidable and hopefully short-term trade-off. Two months later, the stitches are removed. The cornea is looking much healthier and her vision has improved slightly.

As her tumour has been growing it has compressed some of her cranial nerves. We all have twelve pairs of cranial nerves. They arise directly from the brain itself and supply the head, neck, and face, providing sight, hearing, taste, muscle movement and facial sensation. In addition to the visual loss caused by damage to her optic nerve, Olivia's left eye is now unable to look to the left, is dry and has reduced sensation, due to involvement of other cranial nerves. This puts her cornea at permanent risk of further damage. To reduce this risk a referral to Moorfields Eye Hospital in London is arranged and special serum eye drops are prescribed. Made from the liquid part of blood provided by donors, the drops are supplied in small plastic vials that are delivered in batches, packed in dry ice, by special couriers every 2-3 months. The vials must be stored in the freezer and then kept refrigerated during the day of use. Olivia buys a small thermos flask that she packs with ice so that she can safely take a vial with her whenever she leaves her house, thereby ensuring that, wherever she may be, she can apply the drops every 1-2 hours as she has been advised.

As well as involving several cranial nerves, Olivia's tumour is also growing through the base of her skull invading her sinuses and the back of her nose. In the months while she was waiting for her proton therapy, she had developed worsening sinus pressure and blockage of her nasal airways. Although our DIY reflexology sessions in Jacksonville had concentrated on the second, third and fourth toes, the pressure points that correlate with the sinuses, Olivia is still unable to breathe through her nose when we return to the UK. And so it is that, two-months later, she has further surgery to remove tumour from her nose and open her airway. What a joy it is for her to be able to breathe through her nose again.

Olivia has applied to Access to Work, a scheme providing support to those with disabilities so they can get back to, or stay at, work. She is provided with a grant to pay for special voice narrating software and for taxis to take her to and from her office at the university. However, by the time she returns to work in July, her vision has improved to pre-proton levels. She can see well enough to walk to work with her white cane, as the route is familiar to her. Work is certainly more challenging, and things take a bit longer than they used to, but it is great to be back at work with all her friends and colleagues.

Olivia adapts to her new normal. While she was having proton therapy, she had her tiny bathroom converted into a wet room, making it far more accessible for someone with no sight. Although unable to see the plans, she was able to visualise the design she wanted and give clear instructions to the contractors. We are all delighted with the result when we get back to Cambridge.

A kettle that dispenses one-cupful of hot water directly into a mug is purchased so she does not have to take the risk of burning herself when pouring hot water from a traditional kettle. Special oven gloves give her some protection when cooking. Her lodger has moved out which means my wife and I can stay over in the spare bedroom if necessary. We visit from time to time to offer support or to take her to hospital appointments, but Olivia values her independence and is quite able to look after herself.

In September, the status quo is disrupted. Olivia has a heavy nosebleed that cannot be controlled by the traditional means of pinching the nose. Her vision is good enough to see hands moving in front of her face, but she cannot see well enough to determine how much blood she has lost. She is alone and it is scary. As the bleeding does not stop, she attends A&E, where she is joined by her wonderful aunt who lives nearby. I set off from Bristol by car and hope to be with them in the next 3-4 hours. The bleeding is thought to be coming from the tumour at the back of the nose. It settles in A&E, and she is allowed home as I will be there to keep an eye on her. She is given strict instructions to return immediately if she has further bleeding

Two days later, she does have another heavy bleed and we find ourselves back in A&E. One of the on-call ENT surgeons tries to pack her nose to stem the bleeding. He doesn't know Olivia, so I explain that her tumour is high up at the back of her nose and probably out of reach of the packing he is using. Nonetheless, he thinks it is worth trying. Olivia finds it uncomfortable as he packs her left nostril. The bleeding was coming from that side but, as the left nostril is now blocked, blood starts to pour steadily from her right nostril. The doctor starts to pack that side too.

"Won't this mean that the blood will now go down the back of her throat?" I ask anxiously.

This is exactly what happens. Olivia starts gasping and choking. Her nose is blocked by packing so she can only breathe through her mouth. But there is a continuous stream of blood at the back of her mouth that she can't control when she tries to take a breath. It looks as though she is at risk of drowning in her own blood. The doctor has left to book an emergency operating theatre so that Olivia's airway can be protected and packing can be inserted deep enough to stop the bleeding. I shout for help and am about to pull out the packing from her right nostril when the bleeding at last starts to ease and eventually stops. In the early hours of that morning, Olivia undergoes emergency surgery. Afterwards, the consultant who performed the surgery tells me that there was an artery pumping blood from the tumour. He has cauterised the bleeding vessel and packed the rear of Olivia's nose. She must remain an inpatient for 2-days before the packing is removed and she is allowed home.

She continues to have intermittent bleeds over the ensuing months. She is prescribed tablets that encourage the blood to clot. She must start these immediately a bleed begins and so carries them with her at all times. The treatment seems to work. She learns how to manage the bleeding and gradually gains confidence that the episodes will end on their own without further surgical intervention.

The plan had been for Olivia to have a follow-up MRI scan 6-months after returning to the UK to assess the status of her tumour. It is September, and Olivia rings for the result. She is told that the tumour appears a little bit smaller. It is wonderful news. In Jacksonville, her oncologist had told her that there was an 80% chance that the proton therapy would stop her tumour growing further. There was a much lower chance that it would cause it to shrink. Based on this scan result, it appears that the odds are working in Olivia's favour.

Olivia's care at Addenbrookes is provided primarily by the Skull Base Tumour Unit, a multi-disciplinary team that includes oncologists, ENT surgeons, plastic surgeons, neurosurgeons, and specialist nurses. Later that month, Olivia is reviewed by the team. Her scan has been discussed with the radiologists. It appears that the area of tumour that had been removed from the back of her nose earlier in the year has been mistaken for tumour shrinkage. The radiologist had been unaware of this surgery when reporting the scan. On closer inspection, there is a possibility that there has been a slight increase in tumour size inside the brain when compared to the previous scan taken 1-year ago. Although this is not the news we wanted to hear, we rationalise that there was a 4-month gap between last year's scan and the start of the proton therapy. During this time there is sure to have been tumour growth, so the latest scan result does not mean that the proton therapy has failed. Olivia will have to wait for the next follow-up scan, planned in another 6-months' time, to get a better idea of her fate.

## 2020

The new year soon brings new challenges in the shape of the spikey SARS coronavirus-2 and the Covid-19 pandemic. Olivia travels back to Bristol to spend the first lockdown in the family home. For us, it is a surprisingly wondrous time. The weather is unseasonably sunny and warm. There is no car traffic on the country lanes where we live, just cyclists, horse riders and people discovering the pleasure of walking in the countryside. We unearth local walks we never knew about. Olivia relishes the engagement with the natural world around her, and tree hugging becomes an important feature of our walks. She is energised. Determined to get back to her previous levels of fitness, we start going out on runs, tying our wrists together so I can act as her sighted guide.

As lockdown continues, Olivia's sight starts improving. At first, she had needed to hold an arm to be guided on our walks, but now she is able to follow the vague outline of the person in front of her and make her own way with the use of her cane. We don't want to tempt fate but hope that this means her tumour is shrinking.

Her follow-up scan was due in March but has been delayed because of the pandemic. It does take place in July. Olivia learns that the disease is stable. While there has been no tumour shrinkage, nor does there appears to have been any growth. The proton therapy may have worked.

Olivia is now back in Cambridge. All university teaching is being done remotely and she is having to learn how to deliver lectures on-line and have meetings with students over Zoom and Microsoft teams. Through Access to Work, she has obtained funding for a support worker and an ex-student who Olivia had supervised through her Master's degree has taken on this role and is now providing useful assistance.

Olivia's nose is becoming blocked again. She feels that her left eye is bulging out more and there is a firm swelling over her left cheek. Her vision starts deteriorating once more. Given her progressive symptoms, she is not totally surprised to learn that there has been some slight growth of the tumour when she has her next MRI scan in November. Her oncologist tells her that the disease is now 'life limiting', which sounds so much less stark than 'terminal'. As the tumour is slow growing, she is told that the prognosis should be in terms of years rather than months.

## 2021

Olivia accepts her prognosis with grace and fortitude. To those who love her, it seems that she eschews the more typical reactions of fear, anger and sorrow that greet a terminal diagnosis. She is a scientist. Honesty and openness are important components of the scientific method, and she applies these to her current predicament. She realises that she must modify what she hopes for now her future is foreshortened. She no longer hopes to walk in the mountains of Sinai again, but she does still plan to savour the wonders of the natural world by listening to the birdsong in her garden and enjoying the soundscape of walks in the local park. She may not be able to save the world through her pioneering research, but she hopes to continue teaching and inspiring her students, potential researchers of the future. Hope is not lost; it has simply changed.

Olivia's tumour continues to grow. One day in March, she notices a horrible burning smell and her brain seems to go vacant. She does not pass out but is frightened that she may do so. She learns that this is a partial seizure, caused by swelling in the temporal lobe of her brain. It is the first of many similar seizures that she will experience.

Her nose is now completely blocked. She can only breathe through her mouth, which becomes very dry overnight. She is becoming increasingly weary. She begins to sleep during the day. Not just brief naps, but deep sleeps that don't seem to refresh her. The gradual onset of weariness is often the earliest signal of approaching death in people with terminal illnesses. Is this the explanation?

The answer is provided in April when Olivia undergoes further debulking of tumour from the back of her nose. Once she can breathe through her nose again, her energy levels are restored. She throws herself back into life. Enjoying time with family and friends, whenever pandemic rules allow.

But the tumour growth is relentless and, with it, further disabilities ensue. The tumour has invaded her left ear causing complete deafness on that side. It is growing downwards and outwards. Her left eyeball protrudes more and more. The swelling of her left cheek assumes grapefruit size. The tumour invades the roof of her mouth, loosening two teeth, which have to be removed. Speech is becoming difficult and she has lost sensation around her mouth, making eating problematic.

By December, delivering lectures is no longer realistic so Olivia applies for early retirement on health grounds. It will mean that she has more time to focus on finishing her book.

Christmas is to be spent in Northumbria, with brother Tim, Steph, his wife, and their two children Madeleine and newly born Felix. On the way north, Olivia, her mother, and I spend two days visiting York. Supping mulled wine in the Christmas market, attending a carol service in the Minster, and visiting some of Olivia's old haunts from her days undertaking post-doctoral research in York. It is a happy and joyous visit.

Olivia enjoys a sumptuous Christmas lunch and cuddles with her niece and nephew. On Boxing Day, we are joined by her Aunt Clio, who has driven down from Tain, 40 mile north of Inverness, with her dogs. Clio is a prize-winning author who has published eleven historical novels and has been long listed for the Booker prize. She has been acting as a mentor to Olivia, giving advice on the writing of this memoir. Olivia has been sending Clio the latest completed chapters of her book in batches. Each time, Clio has recorded them so that Olivia can listen back to them in instalments. It must have taken a lot of time and is a great kindness.

Olivia struggles with Boxing Day lunch and then crashes immediately after. She goes into a deep sleep, barely rousable and not interested in eating or drinking. We drive her back to Bristol the following day, but there is no improvement in her condition. Fearing the worst, we take her back to Cambridge 2-days later. Her GP visits, the district nursing team is mobilised, and the palliative care team attend to offer their support. It seems that Olivia is nearing the end. So-called 'Just in case' medication is prescribed so that drugs can be administered by a syringe driver if required.

## 2022

Although her medical team thought that she was dying, Olivia has different ideas. She rallies and gets back to finishing her book.

Her nose is blocked once again. She attends her ENT surgeon, a caring and empathic man, who offers to debulk her tumour one more time. As Olivia had so much more energy after the same procedure last year, she readily agrees.

In the interim, her left eye has become more problematic. The bulging is worse and now the conjunctiva is swollen, red and protruding through her closed eyelids. She is referred for an urgent ophthalmological opinion. The surgeon she sees offers to remove her left eye at the same time as the nasal tumour is debulked. By this stage, Olivia has absolutely no vision in that eye. She still has 'visual snow', with tiny, snowflake-like, pixelated bright dots flickering across her entire visual field. In addition, her visual memory at times tricks her into thinking that she can see a resemblance of her hand as she holds it in front of her face. These images are somehow comforting, and she is nervous about how things will be when her eye is removed.

In February, she undergoes the surgery. She now has a glass eye on the right and no eye at all on the left, but her visual snow persists, as does the occasional sense that she can see her own hand moving in front of her. Clearly these symptoms had nothing to do with her damaged eye. They must be false images created by the brain itself.

Although tumour has been removed from her nose, she can still only breathe through her mouth and her energy levels have not improved this time. Her ENT surgeon is disappointed when he reviews her 6-weeks after the surgery. He removes and cauterises some tumour that is protruding from her left ear at this consultation.

Olivia finishes her book at the end of March. She tells me she is worried that without the book she may subconsciously feel there is nothing left to live for and might die. She is gradually sleeping more and more by this time. Speaking and eating are difficult. She has to drink through a straw and can only manage pureed foods fed to her on a spoon. It is infantilising but she does not complain.

She is getting confused at times. On occasions, she struggles to find the right word and she can be a little disinhibited. She records a radio interview about her book. I find it distressing, aware as I am that strangers who listen to the broadcast will not recognise the intelligent and articulate woman that she really is.

Two days after the interview she crashes once more. Deeply asleep for 36-hours, she doesn't take anything in by mouth. Her medical team are remobilised, and we all acknowledge that we have finally reached the end. All of us that is apart from Olivia, who defies us all and again re-emerges from her stupor.

The following evening, I am sat next to her chatting to Tim on the phone. I am describing the roller-coaster ride that she has been on and my inability to come up with any plausible medical explanation.

"It's simple" chips in Olivia. "I just like living".
Maybe it really is as simple and straightforward as that.

*Graduation with dad*

# Afterword
## by
## *Clio Gray (Olivia's aunt)*

My name is Clio Gray. I'm a novelist, and I've been a terrible aunt.

My niece Olivia had a tumour, a retinoblastoma, in one of her eyes that necessitated that eye's removal not long after she was born. I visited several months later. One of very few visits. I've never been a baby person, and took little interest in my sister's children apart from sending home-made if heartfelt presents, like Christmas duvets and knitted figures. Yet now, thirty odd years later, I've learned that Olivia still has the knitted Father Christmas I made her decades ago and still displays it every Christmas, as I do my own.

One of the many things that have moved me since being back in touch with Olivia. Which happened when we knew the tumour had returned for a further bout, and all possible treatments had failed. Olivia then deciding to write about her life, only thirty two years old, contacting me for help. Mad Old Aunt, as I dubbed myself, more than glad – in fact privileged and honoured - to take on the role of Oh Wise Mentor, as Olivia insisted on calling me, which still makes me laugh. Especially considering that the further on we got in the project, even as time was running short, it turned out she didn't really need my help at all. Olivia as good a writer as she has been a liver of life: as vibrant as any of the insects of the Sinai she has documented and surveyed. Including the bee named after her. And how many of us have a bee named after us?

She has astounded me, and astounds me still.

Her name will appear in books of nomenclature for as long as books of nomenclature are written. As will be her name in all the many papers she has written and published, both before and since becoming a Senior Lecturer in Animal and Environmental Biology. She's a marvel. She's her parents' marvel and her brother's, and mine.

Miraculously Olivia, as amazing as always, did revive one more time a few days after Easter and was aware enough to listen to our last voice messages, spend precious time with her family, and got to hold her pre-publication copy of this book. It could not last, and she died a few weeks later.

I will still be the Mad Old Aunt now she is gone, but Olivia will continue to be my own Wise Mentor who has taught me more than anyone to value the small stuff; to try to be as generous, humorous and kind as she was right up to the end.

*Clio with Olivia as a baby*

If you enjoyed this book, please consider leaving
a review at the online bookseller of choice.
Thankyou
and don't forget to check out other
Sparsile titles at www.sparsilebooks.com